The Biochemistry of Energy Utilization in Plants

TERTIARY LEVEL BIOLOGY

A series covering selected areas of biology at advanced undergraduate level. While designed specifically for course options at this level within Universities and Polytechnics, the series will be of great value to specialists and research workers in other fields who require a knowledge of the essentials of a subject.

Recent titles in the series:

Locomotion of Animals	Alexander
Animal Energetics	Brafield and Llewellyn
Biology of Reptiles	Spellerberg
Biology of Fishes	Bone and Marshall
Mammal Ecology	Delany
Virology of Flowering Plants	Stevens
Evolutionary Principles	Calow
Saltmarsh Ecology	Long and Mason
Tropical Rain Forest Ecology	Mabberley
Avian Ecology	Perrins and Birkhead
The Lichen-Forming Fungi	Hawksworth and Hill
Plant Molecular Biology	Grierson and Covey
Social Behaviour in Mammals	Poole
Physiological Strategies in Avian Biology	Phillips, Butler and Sharp
An Introduction to Coastal Ecology	Boaden and Seed
Microbial Energetics	Dawes
Molecule, Nerve and Embryo	Ribchester
Nitrogen Fixation in Plants	Dixon and Wheeler

TERTIARY LEVEL BIOLOGY

The Biochemistry of Energy Utilization in Plants

DAVID T. DENNIS, BSc, PhD
Professor and Head of Biology
Queen's University
Kingston, Ontario

Blackie

Glasgow and London

Published in the USA by
Chapman and Hall
New York

Blackie & Son Limited,
Bishopbriggs, Glasgow G64 2NZ
7 Leicester Place, London WC2H 7BP

Published in the USA by
Chapman and Hall
in association with Methuen, Inc.
29 West 35th Street, New York, NY 10001

British Library Cataloguing in Publication Data

Dennis, David T.
The biochemistry of energy utilization
in plants.—(Tertiary level biology)
1. Photosynthesis 2. Energy transfer
I. Title II. Series
581.1'3342 QK882

ISBN 0–216–91997–5
ISBN 0–216–91998–3 Pbk

Library of Congress Cataloging-in-Publication Data

Dennis, David T.
  The biochemistry of energy utilization in plants.
  (Tertiary level biology)
  Bibliography: p.
  Includes index
  1. Plants—Metabolism. 2. Botanical chemistry.
3. Energy metabolism. I. Title. II. Series.
QK882.D46 1986   581.1'33   86-17532
ISBN 0-412-00981-1 (Chapman and Hall)
ISBN 0-412-00991-9 (Chapman and Hall: pbk.)

Photosetting by Thomson Press (I) Ltd., New Delhi.
Printed in Great Britain by Bell & Bain (Glasgow) Ltd.

Preface

Plants are not easy organisms with which to work. Their cells are surrounded by a tough cell wall that requires harsh measures to disrupt, and this process often leads to an inactivation of the molecules within the cell. Plants also produce large numbers of 'natural products', which will often denature essential cellular molecules. On top of all this, the amounts of proteins, nucleic acids, etc., present in plants are small relative to those in bacteria and animals.

Would it not, therefore, be better simply to leave the field to the animal and bacterial biochemists and trust that plants behave similarly, if not identically, to these organisms? Unfortunately, this is exactly what has happened. Until recently, plants have been regarded as nothing more, biochemically, than green animals, and the only aspect of their metabolism that has been treated independently is photosynthesis.

There is at present a surge of interest in plant biochemistry, as the gaps in our knowledge are seen as a major impediment to progress, especially in such areas as genetic engineering. Techniques for the transfer of genes in plants are well advanced, and the question has become not how to transfer the genes, but which genes should be moved. To be able to answer this question, it is necessary to know the pathways, and to have purified and characterized the enzymes that catalyse these pathways. In the cases that have been studied, fundamental differences between the biochemistry of plants and animals have been found. It is the aim of this book to discuss the subject of plant energetics as it is known now, and to compare our knowledge of plants with that of animals.

I have written this book for students who have some knowledge of biochemistry, such as is covered in the books by Lehninger or Stryer, and have attempted to bridge the gap between these books and the reviews on plant energetics that have appeared in publications such as *Annual Reviews of Plant Physiology*, which often assume a more complete knowledge than is found in elementary books.

I wish to acknowledge the help of Marjory Dennis and Florence Mansfield in drafting the diagrams, and to thank Dave Layzell and Kerry Walsh for reading the manuscript. I would like to thank Queen's University for providing pleasant and hospitable surroundings in which to work, and the Natural Sciences and Engineering Research Council for funding my research over the years.

Finally, I wish to apologize to my wife, Marjory, and to my sons, Roger and Bruce, for my neglect of them while I wrote, and to thank them for their support. It will not happen again—at least, not for two weeks.

DTD

This book is dedicated to my father
THOMAS RICHARD DENNIS
who taught me more than any professor

Contents

CHAPTER ONE

THE NATURE OF ENERGETICS

1.1 Introduction

The second law of thermodynamics states that in a closed system, that is, one isolated from its surroundings, the entropy or randomness of the components of a reaction must always increase. This simple law has led to all kinds of misconceptions about living things; it has even been used to argue that life has special properties that place it outside of normal chemical reactions, and furthermore to indicate that evolution is impossible. The fallacy of this argument lies in the fact that life is not a closed system but must at all times interact with its environment to obtain energy, not only to grow, but also to maintain its complex structure. Without this constant supply of energy in the form of light, reduced inorganic or organic food, an organism would clearly be seen to obey the second law and rapidly disintegrate into randomness.

The basic problem that leads to these misconceptions is the perception of the nature of energy itself, and the manner in which it is presented in textbooks. It is, in fact, much more useful to consider the role of energy in terms of what is important in living systems, namely the equilibrium position of the metabolic reactions. All organisms are ultimately derived from simple materials such as carbon dioxide, inorganic nitrogen and water. These may be obtained directly, as is the case with auxotrophs, or indirectly by heterotrophs through a complex series of interactions in the food chain. Without an input of energy, living organisms would disintegrate into these simple starting materials. In other words, the equilibrium positions of the reactions in the non-living state favour the starting materials. Energy is used to reverse the unfavourable equilibrium of the reactions that make up the pathways of the organism so that its structure can be synthesized and maintained.

1.2 Equilibrium positions of reactions

A metabolic pathway is made up of a series of reactions. For any of these reactions, it is important to determine the equilibrium position. As an example, one reaction that is central to all living organisms is the addition of phosphate to glucose:

glucose + phosphate ↔ glucose 6-phosphate

An examination of this reaction in isolation tells us nothing about its equilibrium position. This is determined by a number of factors. The reaction will tend to move in the direction in which entropy increases and in which enthalpy or heat is lost. A prime consideration, however, is the concentration of the reactants, since any reaction can be made to favour the end products simply by increasing the concentration of the reactants.

Most biochemists are not interested in the details of the mechanism of a reaction, but are more concerned about its overall equilibrium. A measure of the equilibrium position is the free energy change (ΔG) that takes place when a reaction proceeds in either direction. It is related to the enthalpy and entropy changes by the equation

$$\Delta G = \Delta H - T \Delta S$$

where ΔH is the enthalpy change, T is the absolute temperature and ΔS is the entropy change.

The actual free energy change of a reaction is dependent upon the nature of the reaction, the temperature and the concentration of the reactants. In order to be able to compare reactions, the conditions are usually standardized so that the concentration of substrates is considered to be 1 M, the temperature 25° C and the pH 7.0. These exact conditions are never found in a cell, and this must always be kept in mind when discussing cellular reactions. However, under standard conditions reactions can be compared and the free energy change becomes the standard free energy change $\Delta G^{0\prime}$. This is defined as the free energy change that occurs when 1 mole of substrate is converted to 1 mole of product, when all concentrations are at 1 M, except for the hydrogen ion concentration, which is at pH 7.0 (10^{-7} M).

The standard free energy change of the glucose → glucose 6-phosphate reaction is + 13.8 kJ/mol, which means that 13.8 kJ of energy must be supplied to the reaction to convert 1 mole of glucose to glucose 6-phosphate. Or conversely, 13.8 kJ of energy will be liberated when 1 mole of glucose 6-phosphate is converted to inorganic phosphate and glucose.

Reactions will only proceed spontaneously in a direction in which free energy is liberated. Hence, the above reaction will not proceed spontaneously towards glucose 6-phosphate under standard conditions; in fact, under these conditions the reaction in the opposite direction, towards the formation of glucose, is favoured. This does not mean that glucose 6-phosphate cannot be formed under any conditions. For example, if the concentration of glucose and phosphate were exceptionally high, at zero concentration of products, then glucose 6-phosphate could be formed. However, the concentration of glucose and phosphate that would be required to maintain the concentration of glucose 6-phosphate that is normally found in a cell would be very high; outside the range that can be tolerated by a cell, and beyond the solubility of inorganic phosphate.

The main value of knowing $\Delta G^{0\prime}$ is that it is related to the equilibrium constant of the reaction by the equation

$$\Delta G^{0\prime} = 2.3\,RT\log K_{eq}$$

where R is the universal gas constant, T the absolute temperature and K_{eq} the equilibrium constant for the reaction.

We can calculate that the equilibrium position of the above reaction is approximately 7000:1 in favour of glucose and phosphate. If the cell were to maintain glucose 6-phosphate at a concentration of 1 mM and glucose at 10 mM (concentrations that might be expected in animal cells) then the concentration of phosphate would have to be over 1000 M, an impossible value. Obviously, the cell must have a means of overcoming this problem: this forms the whole basis for the study of energetics in both plants and animals.

1.3 The solvent capacity of cells

The above discussion provides an example of the major problem facing living systems. In the cell, simple molecules are converted into complex molecules by a series of reactions known as a metabolic pathway. This can be shown schematically as

$$A \leftrightarrow B \leftrightarrow C \leftrightarrow D \longrightarrow \text{end products}$$

All the reactions are reversible, and the majority will have an equilibrium position that will enable the reaction to proceed in either direction. Although a few may favour the forward direction, many more will favour the starting materials. This overall unfavourable equilibrium of the pathway could be overcome by increasing the concentration of the starting materials. However, enormous concentrations of these metabolites would be required, often beyond their normal solubilities or even the concentrations of the pure compounds, as was shown by the example of glucose 6-phosphate above. A further limitation is the solvent capacity of a cell. Within a cell there are thousands of small molecules in addition to the numerous complex polymers of carbohydrates, proteins and nucleic acids. All these molecules require water in which to dissolve. It has been calculated that, at least in a mitochondrion, there is practically no free water, since all of it is bound to the molecules within the organelle. It has been suggested by Atkinson (1977) that the lack of free water, or the problem associated with the limitation of solvent capacity, is a major hurdle for living systems.

In practice, to overcome this problem of limited solvent capacity, a cell maintains the concentration of starting materials and the intermediates of pathways as low as possible. This means that the equilibrium position of the pathways must be made to favour the end products rather than the starting materials or intermediates. It is the mechanism of keeping these concentrations low that forms the basis of bioenergetics.

1.4 Coupled reactions

The equilibrium position of a reaction cannot be changed in itself, but the objective can be achieved by modifying the reaction by adding components to each side. Consider the following hypothetical reaction:

$$B \leftrightarrow C \quad \text{where} \quad \Delta G^{0\prime} = +5.0 \, \text{kJ/mol} \tag{1}$$

The equilibrium position of this reaction will be far to the left. If we now add the components of the reaction

$$A \leftrightarrow P \quad \text{where} \quad \Delta G^{0\prime} = -10.0 \, \text{kJ/mol} \tag{2}$$

in which the equilibrium lies very far to the right, to each side, the equation becomes

$$A + B \leftrightarrow C + P \quad \text{where} \quad \Delta G^{0\prime} = -5.0 \, \text{kJ/mol} \tag{3}$$

The equilibrium remains in favour of the right-hand side, and the two reactions are said to be coupled. The highly favourable equilibrium of (2) enables the equilibrium of (3) to favour the end products, allowing the production of C from B.

If in turn A can be regenerated from P, we obtain the following sequence of reactions in which single arrows are used to indicate the equilibrium positions of the reactions:

$$A + B \rightarrow C + P$$
$$P \rightarrow A$$

<hr>

$$B \rightarrow C$$

<hr>

The equilibrium position of reaction (1) has now been made to favour the product C. Although reactions (1) and (2) are said to be coupled, they can only be separated in theory. In the cell they would occur as one reaction, as shown in (3). Many of the reactions in the cell are of this nature, so that the overall equilibrium position of the biosynthetic pathways can be made to favour the cellular products.

1.5 Phosphate as an intermediate

In all living organisms, phosphate is used as an intermediate in the majority of coupled reactions. There are many properties of phosphate that uniquely suit it for this role. In the first place, phosphoric acid will form an acid anhydride bond with itself to give pyrophosphate (PPi). This is unstable and will hydrolyse back to inorganic phosphate (Pi), the equilibrium position being in favour of inorganic phosphate:

$$PPi + H_2O \leftrightarrow 2Pi \quad \Delta G^{0\prime} = -31 \text{ kJ/mol}$$

Phosphoric acid will also form mixed acid anhydrides with other acids that are even more unstable than pyrophosphate itself:

$$\overset{\displaystyle O}{\overset{\displaystyle \|}{R-C}}-O-P+H_2O \leftrightarrow \overset{\displaystyle O}{\overset{\displaystyle \|}{R-C}}OH+Pi \quad \Delta G^{0\prime} = -49 \text{ kJ/mol}$$

In addition to forming acid anhydride bonds, phosphate can readily form esters with a whole range of alcohols that are more stable than the acid anhydrides:

$$R-O-P+H_2O \leftrightarrow R-OH+Pi \quad \Delta G^{0\prime} = -14 \text{ kJ/mol}$$

Phosphate can also form compounds with sulphur and nitrogen. It is the versatility of phosphate in combining with a whole range of compounds that makes it of such great importance in living organisms. Of even greater relevance, however, are the great differences in the standard free energy of hydrolysis of the various phosphate compounds that enable phosphate to act as an intermediate in many chemical reactions. It is difficult to imagine life without phosphate, just as it is impossible to visualize life without carbon. No other molecule has the versatile properties of phosphate for energy coupling.

1.6 Adenosine triphosphate

Inorganic phosphate is present in all cells and plays a vital role in metabolism. Certain organisms, such as some bacteria and possibly all plants, also use inorganic pyrophosphate as an energy source. However, in most cases pyrophosphate is not used itself, in coupled reactions, but is linked to adenosine through a third phosphate to form adenosine triphosphate (ATP) (Figure 1.1). It must be recognized, however, that it is the terminal pyrophosphate group that is involved in the majority of reactions. The free energy of hydrolysis of the terminal acid anhydride bond is not significantly different from that of pyrophosphate itself.

In many reactions ATP acts as a phosphoryl donor, donating the terminal phosphate to a series of compounds and leaving as a product adenosine diphosphate (ADP). Hence, in the reaction discussed earlier ATP donates its terminal phosphate to glucose to form glucose 6-phosphate in a reaction that is catalysed by the enzyme hexokinase:

$$ATP + glucose \leftrightarrow glucose\ 6\text{-}phosphate + ADP$$

The $\Delta G^{0'}$ for this reaction is $-17\,kJ/mol$ and can be thought of as being

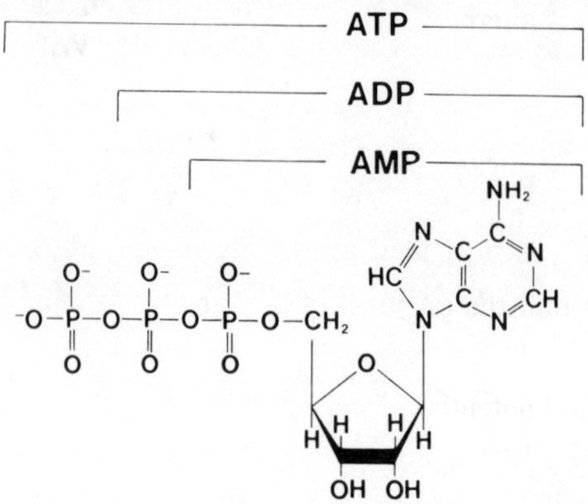

Figure 1.1   The structure of adenosine triphosphate (ATP). The structures of adenosine diphosphate (ADP) and adenosine monophosphate (AMP) are also indicated.

made up of two reactions:

$$\text{glucose} + \text{Pi} \leftrightarrow \text{glucose 6-phosphate} + H_2O \quad \Delta G^{0'} = +14\,\text{kJ/mol}$$

$$\text{ATP} + H_2O \leftrightarrow \text{ADP} + \text{Pi} \quad \Delta G^{0'} = -31\,\text{kJ/mol}$$

It should be remembered, however, that the reaction occurs on the surface of the enzyme and the phosphate is transferred directly from the ATP to the glucose.

The second bond in ATP can also be hydrolysed with a similar free energy of hydrolysis to the first one to yield adenosine monophosphate (AMP) and pyrophosphate. In some reactions this acid anhydride bond is used. However, hydrolysis of the third bond with the formation of AMP is accompanied by a smaller free energy change since this is an ester bond.

The acid anhydride bond in ATP is often referred to as a high-energy bond. This is inaccurate usage since, in chemistry, a high-energy bond is a stable bond, quite the opposite from the bond in ATP. Similarly, ATP is often called a high-energy compound. This is more acceptable, but it still can lead to some confusion. To be effective as an intermediate in energy reactions, not only must ATP be able to donate a phosphate to other compounds, but also it must be possible to reform ATP from ADP and Pi. The free energy of hydrolysis must, therefore, occupy an intermediate position. It must be high enough for it to act as a phosphoryl donor but not too high to prevent ADP from accepting a phosphate and reforming ATP.

The high free energy of hydrolysis of ATP results from a number of factors. The first, and most important, is the stabilization of the products, especially Pi, by resonance. Resonance in ATP is reduced because of the limitation imposed by the acid anhydride bond. When the terminal phosphate is released the potential for resonance is greatly increased, making the products much more stable. The second factor contributing to the instability is the proximity of similar charges within the ATP molecule. Likewise, the repulsion of the charges on ADP and Pi inhibit their combination. Finally, on hydrolysis a proton is released which at pH 7.0 tends to pull the reaction in favour of hydrolysis.

1.7 The phosphate potential or energy charge

The two terminal acid anhydride bonds in ATP have a high free energy of hydrolysis. The system can be described by the following equation:

$$\text{ATP} \leftrightarrow \text{ADP} + \text{Pi} \leftrightarrow \text{AMP} + \text{Pi}$$

It can be compared with a battery that can be either fully charged (all the adenylate as ATP) or fully discharged (all the adenylate as AMP). Atkinson (1977) has suggested that when all the adenylate is present as ATP the energy charge should have a value of 1. When it is all present as AMP then the charge should be 0. The importance of ATP in maintaining the integrity of a cell can be judged from the fact that, in a healthy cell, the energy charge is always controlled at a value of between 0.8 and 0.9; in other words, most of the adenylates are present as ATP. At values significantly below this the cell dies.

A discussion of the energetics of living systems is in reality a description of coupled reactions. Energy is supplied by sunlight and, through a series of coupled reactions, is ultimately used in biosynthetic pathways in both plants and animals to reverse reactions with unfavourable equilibria so that the overall equilibrium of a pathway favours the end product. The most commonly used molecule involved in the transfer of energy in these coupled reactions is ATP, so that energetics can be reduced essentially to two components. In the first place, it is necessary to describe the mechanism by which ATP is involved in the reaction of enzymes. Secondly, it is important to investigate the means by which ATP can be resynthesized from ADP and inorganic phosphate.

The synthesis of ATP in turn can be considered to be composed of two parts. In the first place, ATP is synthesized directly, utilizing the energy derived from sunlight in the process of photosynthesis which occurs in plants and some prokaryotes. Secondly, in animals, in plants in the dark, and in non-photosynthetic prokaryotes, ATP synthesis is coupled to the degradation of either ingested or stored food material. In this latter process, the complex molecules of the food material are degraded to simple molecules, carbon dioxide and water. Therefore, even though the complex molecule, ATP, is formed and subsequently used to synthesize other complex molecules, the overall entropy of the system increases.

In all the processes of energetics, some of the most fundamental reactions involve the transfer of electrons in what are referred to as oxidation–reduction reactions. The initial reactions of photosynthesis result in the synthesis of highly reduced compounds. Hence, the understanding of energetics requires a knowledge of oxidation–reduction reactions and these are discussed in the next chapter.

More detailed information on the topics covered in this chapter can be found in, for example, Goodwin and Mercer (1983), Lehninger (1971), Morowitz (1978), Morris (1974), Smith *et al.* (1983) and Stryer (1981).

CHAPTER TWO

OXIDATION–REDUCTION REACTIONS

2.1 Introduction

Reactions involving the transfer of electrons from one compound to another are of the most fundamental importance in all living systems. Photosynthesis generates compounds that are powerful reducing agents, and from them electrons are transferred through a series of compounds ultimately to oxygen in either animal or plant mitochondria.

Oxidation–reduction reactions involve the transfer of electrons from the reductant, which is oxidized in the process, to the oxidant which is reduced. It is the transfer of the electron or electrons that is the essential part of the reaction, even though hydrogen atoms or hydride ions may in fact be the actual unit that is moved. Oxidation–reduction reaction may take the following forms in living systems:

(i) The transfer of an electron between two metal ions that may be bound into a biological molecule, for example

$$Fe^{2+} + Cu^{2+} \leftrightarrow Fe^{3+} + Cu^{+}$$

(ii) The transfer of hydrogen atoms from the reductant to the oxidant, for example

$$DH_2 + A \leftrightarrow D + AH_2$$

where D is a donor molecule and A is an acceptor.

(iii) The transfer of a hydride ion (H^-, equivalent to H^+ plus $2e^-$), for example

$$\underset{\substack{|\\COO^-}}{\overset{\substack{R\\|}}{H-C-O-H}} + A^+ \leftrightarrow \underset{\substack{|\\COO^-}}{\overset{\substack{R\\|}}{C=O}} + AH + H^+$$

9

(iv) Finally, the transfer of electrons from a substrate to oxygen:

$$O_2 + 4H^+ + 4e^- \leftrightarrow 2H_2O$$

2.2 Redox potential

Within living systems there exists a whole range of compounds that have different affinities for electrons. Compounds that bind electrons loosely and readily transfer them to other molecules are reducing agents; compounds that bind electrons tightly and remove them from other molecules are oxidizing agents.

The affinity of a compound for an electron is termed its redox potential, and can be measured in volts. The actual redox potential of a molecule depends not just on the affinity of the molecule for electrons but also on the concentration of the reduced and oxidized forms of the molecule, in what is known as a *redox pair*.

In order to make it possible to compare molecules it is necessary to measure their affinity for electrons under standard conditions. Ideally these are the conditions when the concentration of the oxidized and reduced forms are equal and at 1 M concentration. In practice, most redox potentials are measured when the two concentrations are simply equal and not 1 M.

One cannot discuss a redox potential in isolation; there must be a compound that accepts electrons and one that donates electrons. There must also be a standard against which everything else is measured. The standard that has been chosen is that of the hydrogen electrode. In this reaction, hydrogen gas reacts with an electron acceptor to form protons and a reduced electron acceptor. To make the reaction standard the hydrogen gas should be at 1 atm pressure and the proton concentration must be 1 M (i.e. zero pH). The loss of electrons by hydrogen can be described by the equation

$$H_2 \leftrightarrow 2H^+ + 2e^-$$

To construct a standard electrode one could, therefore, take an aqueous solution at pH zero over which there is hydrogen gas at atmospheric pressure and into which is inserted a platinum electrode. This electrode is arbitrarily given the potential of 0 V. To measure the potential of any other redox pair one could then construct a second electrode consisting of equal amounts of the reduced and oxidized forms of the compound. When the electrodes in each solution are connected, a

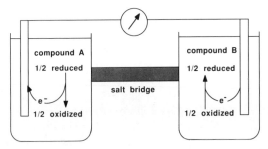

Figure 2.1   An apparatus for comparing the standard or midpoint potentials of two redox couples. If one of these electrodes was a hydrogen electrode, then it would contain an aqueous solution at pH 0 and would be equilibrated with an atmosphere of hydrogen gas at one atmosphere pressure.

potentiometer could be used to determine whether electrons tend to flow to the hydrogen electrode or away from it and the potential difference between the two electrodes could be measured. Since the hydrogen electrode is given a potential of 0 V, the potential of the second electrode could be found. A scheme for such an experiment is shown in Figure 2.1.

In fact, such a simple system rarely works. For one thing, biological molecules will usually not react with a platinum electrode so that this procedure is of much more interest to the inorganic chemist. We are also not used to considering living cells at zero pH, but rather at pH 7.0, under which conditions the hydrogen electrode has a redox potential of -4.2 volts since the H^+ concentration is now 10^{-7} which pulls the above reaction to the right. How can we then measure the redox potential of biological molecules?

As in the case of free energy, biologists are really more interested in the equilibrium position of a reaction than in measuring its exact chemical parameters. When two compounds are mixed together, electrons will be passed from one to the other until the system comes to equilibrium. If each redox couple is initially at equal concentrations of oxidized and reduced forms, then electrons will be passed from the couple with the more negative potential to the couple with the more positive potential. Under standard conditions the equilibrium position of the reaction is related to the difference between the two redox potentials by the equation

$$\Delta E'_0 = 2.3\,RT/nF \cdot \log K_{eq}$$

where $\Delta E'_0$ is the difference in the standard redox potential between the two redox couples, F is the Faraday constant and n is the number of electrons transferred. Hence, in practical terms the redox potential is measured by allowing the reaction to go to equilibrium, then measuring the concentration of the reactants from which the standard redox potential can be calculated.

In the cell, standard conditions are rarely, if ever, found and the components of a redox couple will not be at equal concentrations. In fact, it seems necessary for a cell to keep some compounds highly reduced whereas others seem to be kept fully oxidized.

2.3 Electron carriers in cells

2.3.1 Introduction

A cell needs various types of electron carrier (see Goodwin and Mercer (1983), Smith *et al.* (1983), Stryer (1981)). It must have mobile carriers in the cytosol that can interact with soluble components and be involved in the transfer of reducing equivalents both between the soluble molecules and also between the various organelles. Within the organelles there are electron carriers in the soluble phase of the organelle, but there are also membrane-associated electron carriers. These may be soluble in the bilayer of the membrane or may be associated with large protein complexes.

2.3.2 Soluble electron carriers

There are two soluble electron carriers in the cells of both plants and animals, NAD and NADP, whose structure is shown in Figure 2.2. The essential component in the oxidation–reduction reaction is the nicotinamide ring. On reduction this ring accepts a hydride ion or two reducing equivalents to form the quinone structure as shown in the diagram. Hence in a typical reaction malate is oxidized to oxalocetic acid and the NAD^+ is reduced to NADH:

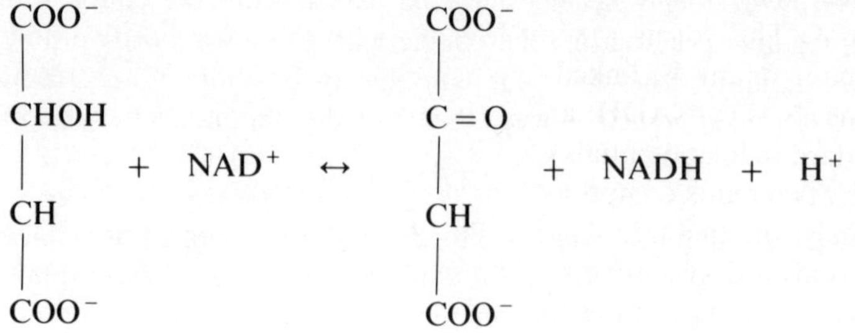

$$
\begin{array}{l}
COO^- \\
| \\
CHOH \\
| \qquad + \ NAD^+ \ \leftrightarrow \\
CH \\
| \\
COO^-
\end{array}
\qquad
\begin{array}{l}
COO^- \\
| \\
C = O \\
| \qquad + \ NADH \ + \ H^+ \\
CH \\
| \\
COO^-
\end{array}
$$

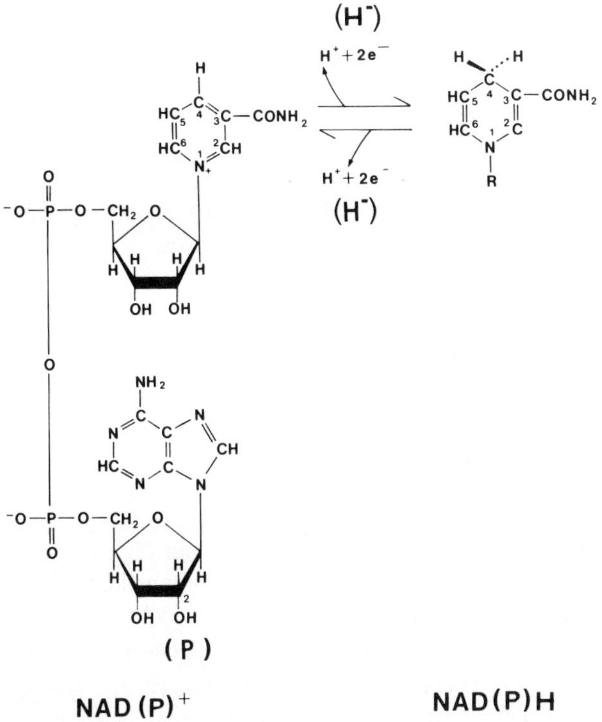

Figure 2.2 The structure of NAD^+. The structure of the nicotinamide part of the molecule of the reduced form of NAD^+, NADH, is also shown. The position of the phosphate group on the 2' position of the ribose in $NADP^+$ is indicated by (P).

In this reaction a proton is released, and this must be considered in the overall reaction. At pH 7.0 the reaction is pulled to the right by the low concentrations of protons, a situation that is likely to occur in the cell. The state of reduction of both NAD and NADP can readily be determined because the reduced form absorbs in the UV part of the spectrum at 340 nM. This forms a simple assay for many enzymes that use these cofactors or can be linked to enzymes that use them.

The NAD^+/NADH and $NADP^+$/NADPH couples have identical standard redox potentials of -0.32 V; the question that naturally follows is why two redox compounds are needed. It appears to be a general rule in animals, and to a large extent in plants, that the NAD^+/NADH couple is involved in degradative reactions. Hence, NAD^+ is reduced during the oxidation of metabolites that are being broken down. The NADH that is formed is then itself oxidized during the generation of ATP from ADP and inorganic phosphate. In contrast, the $NADP^+$/NADPH couple is involved in biosynthetic reactions in which oxidized metabolites are being reduced to components that are required by the cell. The use of different electron carriers means that biosynthetic and degradative reactions can be kept separate. Why should this be important?

The answer to this question is related to the difference between the standard redox potential discussed above and the actual redox potential that the couple may have in the cell. Through the mechanism of the regulatory control of the enzymes involved in the metabolism of NAD and NADP, the NAD^+/NADH couple is kept 90% oxidized, whereas the $NADP^+$/NADPH couple is kept 90% reduced. This means that in the cell the actual redox potential of the NAD^+/NADH couple is approximately -0.29 V, whereas that of the $NADP^+$/NADPH couple is -0.35 V. In the cell, therefore, the $NADP^+$/NADPH couple is a better reducing agent. This means that biosynthetic reactions have an equilibrium position that is more in favour of the synthetic reaction than might have been predicted from the standard redox potential, and conversely degradative reactions are more in favour of degradation.

The nicotinamide part of the molecule is identical in NAD and NADP. The rest of the molecule in each case is used for identification in the cell, so that enzymes can specifically bind one or the other. The majority of enzymes are specific for one of these cofactors, although some exceptions are known. In plants, the general rule that NAD is used for degradative reactions and NADP for synthetic reactions, holds true for the most part, although there are some notable exceptions which will be discussed later. This unexpected use of NAD results from the more complex nature of plant metabolism.

So far, these two reductants have been discussed in relation to the metabolism of the cytosol. It must be realized, however, that they are also important in metabolism within the aqueous compartments of organelles. The reduction of $NADP^+$ to NADPH is one of the principal functions of photosynthesis. The NADPH is subsequently used in the reductive reactions of photosynthesis which result in carbon dioxide being reduced to carbohydrate. Although NADP is the principal compound involved in redox reactions in the chloroplast, NAD is also found in this organelle and appears to be necessary for fatty acid biosynthesis. In the mitochondrion, NAD^+ is the soluble oxidant used in the tricarboxylic acid cycle where it functions in the transfer of electrons from the soluble reactions to the membrane-bound reactions of the electron transport chain.

2.3.3 Membrane-associated electron-transfer compounds

2.3.3.1 Electron transport chains. So far we have considered only electron transfer compounds that are soluble in either the cytosol or the aqueous phase of an organelle. The majority of electron transfer compounds are immobilized, at least to some extent, in membranes. This association with membranes allows the sequential transfer of electrons between the components of the membrane so that the whole acts as a chain. This means that the energy is released in discrete amounts as the electrons are passed from component to component, instead of the whole of the free energy change being accomplished at one time. The nature of the electron transport chains in the chloroplast and the mitochondrion will be discussed later. It must be remembered, however, that there are other electron transport chains, for example in the endoplasmic reticulum, which are involved in reactions such as hydroxylations.

A second reason for the incorporation of electron transfer components into a membrane is that it allows reactions to occur across a membrane. For example, protons are transported across the membrane during electron transfer both in mitochondria and in chloroplasts. Electron transport chains may also be used in the uptake of nutrients into cells.

2.3.3.2 The iron–sulphur centres. The electron transport chains of the mitochondrion and the chloroplast contain a large number of iron–sulphur centres that have been difficult to study because they are unstable and cannot be isolated (see Palmer (1975) for a review). The iron–sulphur centres are single electron transfer compounds in which the iron atom undergoes a reversible valency change from Fe(II) to Fe(III). They are protein molecules into which are bound either two or four iron atoms. The iron atoms are covalently attached to the protein through the sulphur atoms of cysteine residues in the protein. Also linking the iron atoms are sulphur atoms that are unstable and can be released from the iron–sulphur centre as hydrogen sulphide on acidification of the molecule.

The iron–sulphur centres are not easy to study. They cannot be extracted and studied *in vitro*; neither can they be readily studied *in vivo*, because they do not have a distinctive absorption spectrum that changes on oxidation and reduction—as do many of the other electron transfer compounds. Most data on iron–sulphur compounds have been obtained by electron spin resonance spectrophotometry (ESR). This technique detects unpaired electrons in molecules, since an unpaired electron has a spin that is not balanced by a second electron in the same orbital having a compensating opposite spin. Such unpaired electrons can reverse their spin by absorbing microwave radiation, and hence can be detected. Most of the iron–sulphur centres only show an ESR signal on reduction. One group of iron–sulphur proteins, however—the high-potential iron proteins or HiPIP centres— give a signal only in the oxidized state.

Many iron–sulphur centres have been detected by ESR. It must always be remembered, however, that these centres are really only signals in a spectrophotometer. How these signals relate to the actual structure of the membrane cannot be determined directly. Also, distinctive signals can only be obtained at very low temperatures, that is, below 100°K, so that the tissue must be specially prepared to detect them.

2.3.3.3 The cytochromes. The cytochromes are proteins of low molecular weight containing a porphyrin-type molecule, commonly called a haem, into which is bound an iron atom. Cytochromes undergo single-electron oxidation–reduction changes in which the iron atom reversibly changes its valency state from Fe(II) to Fe(III). The majority of cytochromes are membrane-bound, and they can be very hydrophobic. An exception is cytochrome *c*, which associates with the surface of the mitochondrial inner membrane and is water-soluble.

The cytochromes of plant mitochondria and chloroplasts are divided into three groups termed *a*, *b* and *c* type cytochromes. All cytochromes in the reduced state have three distinctive absorbance peaks in the visible region of the spectrum. The three types of cytochrome can be distinguished by the wavelengths at which these absorbance peaks occur. The haem group in the *a* cytochromes differs from that found in the *b* and *c* type cytochromes. In the *c* type cytochromes the haem is covalently bound to the protein, and cannot be readily removed by denaturation of protein. In many cytochromes the iron atom is coordinately bound by four bonds to the haem molecule. In some cytochromes such as *c* types the fifth and sixth coordinate positions of the iron are associated with the protein, whereas in the *a* type cytochromes the sixth position is free, allowing the molecule to react with oxygen or carbon monoxide.

Hence, although the cytochromes are classed together as a group of electron-transfer compounds, they are quite distinctive in many of their features and are involved in quite specific and unique reactions in the cell. The standard redox potential of the different cytochromes can also be very different. For further details see Goodwin and Mercer (1983), Pradet and Raymond (1983), Chapter 4, Smith *et al.* (1983), Stryer (1981).

2.3.3.4 The flavins. There are two flavins involved in redox reactions in cells, flavin mononucleotide (FMN) and flavin adenine dinucleotide (FAD) (see Forti, 1977). Both are tightly bound prosthetic groups of enzymes. The active electron-transfer portion of both molecules is the flavin moiety that can accept two hydrogen atoms from a substrate to form $FMNH_2$ or $FADH_2$. The flavins are therefore similar, in some ways, to the pyridine nucleotide electron-transfer compounds, but they differ in a fundamental respect. NAD and NADP are highly mobile in the soluble phases of the cell, and act to transfer reducing equivalents between molecules and various cell compartments. In contrast, the flavin electron carriers are firmly bound to proteins and are often components of large complexes. The flavins are, therefore, restricted with respect to the molecules with which they can interact.

The flavin electron carriers are involved in two distinct types of reaction. Some flavoproteins catalyse the transfer of electrons from a substrate to oxygen. In this case the flavin group must be at the surface of the protein to allow the interaction with oxygen. In other cases, the flavin moiety is encased in the protein to prevent this interaction with oxygen. In this second type the transfer of electrons occurs only between substrates and acceptors. Why some enzymes contain FMN whereas others have FAD is not clear: the standard redox potential of the two is the virtually the same.

2.3.3.5 Ubiquinone and plastoquinone. Ubiquinone and plastoquinone are similar in structure (see Goodwin and Mercer (1983), Morowitz (1978), Chapter 1, Smith *et al.* (1983) and Stryer (1981).) They both have a quinone ring system carrying a long isoprene side chain that renders the molecule soluble in lipids. They can be reduced by the acceptance of two hydrogen atoms to form the dihydroquinones. Therefore, these molecules have similarities to the flavins and pyridine electron carriers. These electron-transfer compounds act as mobile carriers within the lipid phase of the membranes of the mitochondrion in the case of ubiquinone, and the chloroplast in the case of plastoquinone, linking the large immobile protein complexes in these membranes and transferring electrons between them.

Although the overall reaction of the quinones is to accept two hydrogen atoms, it has been suggested that in the membrane of the organelle the quinone may at times accept only a single electron to form a free radical or semiquinone. These free radicals can be detected by ESR and they may play a very important role in the cell metabolism even though the lifetime of the semiquinone is short.

2.3.3.6 Conclusions. It is clear that cells contain a wide variety of electron-transfer compounds. These different compounds play distinctive roles in the metabolism of the cell. Some have the role of mobile carriers of electrons between the molecules of the soluble phases of the cell, whereas others play the same role within the hydrophobic domains of the membranes. Other electron carriers are immobilized constituents of cell membranes where they form components of electron-transport chains and may have the additional function of transferring reducing equivalents vectorially across the membrane. Finally, a variety of compounds are required to span the wide range of redox potentials that are required by living systems.

The material covered in this chapter is reviewed in more detail in Goodwin and Mercer (1983), Lehninger (1971), Morowitz (1978), Morris (1974), Smith *et al.* (1983) and Stryer (1981).

CHAPTER THREE

MECHANISMS OF ENERGY TRANSDUCTION

3.1 Introduction

Energy transduction is one of the most fascinating areas of plant metabolism, and a large amount of research effort has been directed towards the elucidation of the mechanisms by which the various processes take place. The term transduction refers to the conversion of one form of energy into another, such as the use of light energy to generate ATP from ADP in the chloroplast. However, this research is difficult because the reactions involved are complex and usually require an organized structure. For example, the bulk of the ATP synthesis occurs in the mitochondrion and requires the integrity of the inner membrane of the organelle to be intact. Hence, one cannot study mitochondrial ATP synthesis as one would study an enzyme, since an enzyme can be purified and treated as a normal chemical catalyst. Instead, numerous components are involved, and, although the study of each one independently may be useful, it can lead to misconceptions or to information that is irrelevant or impossible to integrate into a coherent picture. In this section we will discuss the synthesis of ATP as a prime example of energy transduction.

The synthesis of ATP is coupled to various oxidation–reduction reactions. The basic question that needs to be elucidated, therefore, is how the energy that is made available during an oxidation–reduction reaction is used to synthesize ATP from ADP and inorganic phosphate, remembering from Chapter 1 that the equilibrium position of this reaction favours ADP and phosphate. This has been a major problem facing biochemists for many years, especially in the mitochondrion and the chloroplast where the bulk of ATP synthesis occurs in plant cells. In these organelles ATP synthesis is associated with the oxidation–reduction reactions that occur in the membranes of the organelles where the electron–transport chains are found.

3.2 Substrate-level phosphorylation

The earliest attempts at describing energy transduction used, as a model, the mechanism by which ATP is synthesized in the reactions of cellular metabolism (see Dennis, 1983). This is referred to as substrate-level phosphorylation, since the actual substrates of the reaction are directly involved in the formation of ATP. A major site of substrate level phosphorylation is the glycolytic pathway, which will be described in more detail later. ATP generation by this pathway is essential under anaerobic conditions, when the production of ATP in the mitochondrion is inhibited by the lack of oxygen.

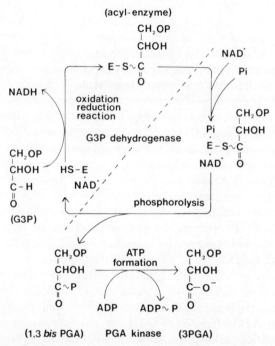

Figure 3.1 Substrate-level phosphorylation as demonstrated by the reactions catalysed by glyceraldehyde 3-phosphate dehydrogenase and phosphoglycerate kinase. The partial reaction of glyceraldehyde 3-phosphate dehydrogenase involving the oxidation of glyceraldehyde 3-phosphate with the formation of a thioester bond between 3-phosphoglycerate and an —SH on the enzyme is shown to the left of the dotted line. The partial reaction to right of the dotted line shows the formation of the mixed acid anhydride between 3-phosphoglycerate and phosphate. In all cases a ∼ bond indicates a bond with a high free energy of hydrolysis. (Adapted from Dennis, 1983.)

A typical substrate-level reaction is that catalysed by the enzymes glyceraldehyde 3-phosphate dehydrogenase and 3-phosphoglycerate kinase, which together catalyse the reactions shown in Figure 3.1. In the initial part of the first reaction, catalysed by glyceraldehyde 3-phosphate dehydrogenase, glyceraldehyde 3-phosphate is oxidized to the level of 3-phosphoglycerate with the concomitant reduction of NAD^+. The 3-phosphoglycerate, however, is not released from the enzyme but remains bound to it through a thioester bond. The NADH that is produced in the reaction can be transported to the mitochondrion and used for ATP synthesis. However, there is still energy available for more ATP synthesis because of the thioester bond that is formed during the reaction. More importantly, this ATP can be synthesized even in the absence of oxygen when the mitochondrial system is inactive.

Thioester bonds are very unstable; that is, they have a high negative free energy of hydrolysis. The thioester bond between 3-phosphoglycerate and the enzyme glyceraldehyde 3-phosphate dehydrogenase could be hydrolysed by water to yield 3-phosphoglycerate. The equilibrium of this reaction would be very much in favour of the products. However, in the second part of the reaction catalysed by glyceraldehyde 3-phosphate dehydrogenase, the thioester bond is cleaved by phosphoric acid instead of water to yield the product 1, 3-bisphosphoglycerate. In this case, most of the energy made available during the reaction is conserved by the formation of the mixed acid anhydride bond between phosphoric acid and 3-phosphoglycerate, and the overall reaction is reversible.

In the second reaction, catalysed by phosphoglycerate kinase, the mixed acid anhydride bond of 1,3-bisphosphoglycerate is cleaved but this time ADP instead of water is involved in the cleavage, and the phosphate is transferred to the ADP with the formation of ATP. Considering the two reactions together, therefore, glyceraldehyde 3-phosphate is oxidized to 3-phosphoglycerate with the reduction of NAD^+. In the process, ADP and phosphate are combined to produce ATP. Hence, in this substrate-level phosphorylation, the oxidation–reduction reaction is directly involved in the synthesis of ATP.

It was thought for a long time that all ATP synthesis occurred by a process analogous to that described for the above reactions. The fundamental problem that remained was to identify an intermediate with a high negative free energy of hydrolysis analogous to 1,3-bisphosphoglycerate. A large amount of research effort and many millions of dollars were spent on trying to find such intermediates in the mitochondrion. However, after several false alarms it was finally decided that no such intermediate existed.

3.3 The chemiosmotic coupling theory

In 1961 Mitchell put forward a theory of energy transduction in mito-chondria and chloroplasts that did not require an intermediate with a high free energy of hydrolysis. At the time, however, the biochemical community was so wedded to the idea of substrate-level phosphorylation that his ideas received scant recognition. The theory, often called the chemiosmotic theory, accepted that no high-energy intermediate existed but suggested instead that the energy was conserved as an electrochemical gradient across a membrane. In the case of the mitochondrion, it was suggested that this gradient occurred across the inner membrane and would then be used in a second reaction for the formation of ATP. This scheme, or variations of it, is now accepted as the means by which ATP is synthesized in both mitochondria and chloroplasts. For more detailed reviews, see Chance (1977), Dennis (1983), Ernster (1977), Mitchell (1961), (1966), Nicholls (1982), Racker (1977), Williams (1978).

In Mitchell's scheme the actual synthesis of ATP is separated from the oxidation–reduction reactions of the components that comprise the electron-transport chain. He postulated that the synthesis of ATP occurred on an enzyme that had been shown to exist in mitochondria, but for which at that time no function had been found. The enzyme in question was an ATPase, that is, an enzyme which when extracted from the organelle catalyses the hydrolysis of ATP to ADP and inorganic phosphate. Because of the high free energy of hydrolysis of ATP, the equilibrium position of this reaction is very much in favour of the products. Why was such an enzyme present in the mitochondrion, an organelle that has the function of ATP synthesis?

Mitchell proposed that the ATPase was involved in ATP synthesis and should, in fact, be called ATP synthase. All enzyme reactions are reversible, so that when the ATP synthase is isolated from the mitochondrion it catalyses the hydrolysis of ATP since the equilibrium favours this reaction. In the mitochondrion the situation is quite different. The ATP synthase is bound into the inner membrane of the organelle, and is not free in solution like most enzymes.

One of the most important concepts developed by Mitchell was the idea of vectorial processes in cells (see Mitchell, 1976; 1977). There are many enzymes that are bound into membranes. Every enzyme has a binding site for substrates as well as for the products of the reaction. It is possible that, when an enzyme is bound into a membrane, these two sites are spatially separated so that the substrate binding site is on one side of the membrane

whereas the product releasing site is on the opposite. Therefore, there may
be not only catalysis of a reaction, but also be transport of a component of
the reaction across the membrane. Mitchell postulated that the electron-
transport chain in the inner membrane of the mitochondrion was organized
across the membrane in such a manner that, as electrons passed down the
chain, protons were absorbed inside the organelle and released outside. The
inner membrane of the mitochondrion is impermeable to protons, so that
as the electron-transport chain moves protons across the membrane a

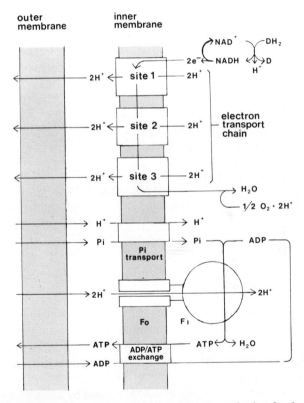

Figure 3.2 A schematic representation of the chemiosmotic mechanism for the formation
of ATP in the mitochondrion. The oxidation of NADH by the electron transport chain
and ultimately oxygen is shown, as are the three sites of proton transport in the electron
transport chain. The synthesis of ATP coupled to proton transport associated with the ATP
synthase (F_0 and F_1) is also indicated. The uptake of phosphate into the mitochondrial
matrix and the exchange of ATP and ADP is shown. This scheme is based on the work of
Mitchell (1961), (1966), (1972), (1976), (1977). (Adapted from Dennis, 1983.)

gradient develops, in which there is a high concentration outside the mitochondrion relative to that in the matrix. This gradient acts as the intermediate energy store, replacing the chemical intermediate that had been postulated earlier.

How is this store of energy in the form of a proton gradient used to synthesize ATP? Mitchell postulated that the ATP synthase is also located across the membrane, in such a manner that the catalytic site faces into the matrix of the mitochondrion where the enzyme catalyses the synthesis of ATP from ADP. This reaction requires the input of energy which is provided by the proton gradient. To utilize the energy of this gradient, Mitchell suggested that the ATP synthase was not only an enzyme but also a proton transporter.

The synthase is a complex molecule consisting of the catalytic site which protrudes into the matrix and a portion that is incorporated into the membrane. This membrane portion contains a proton channel and is one of the few places where protons can re-enter the matrix. Mitchell postulated that when ADP and phosphate are bound to the ATP synthase, two protons could pass through this channel and to the catalytic site. This movement of protons would discharge the proton gradient and result in a release of energy that could be used to reverse the normal equilibrium of the ATP synthase reaction. Hence, ATP would be synthesized. This is shown schematically in Figure 3.2. From these considerations of the storage of energy as a proton gradient, Mitchell (1976) developed the concept of proticity. This is analogous to electricity, since protons are highly mobile in water and similar to the highly mobile electrons in a metal.

3.4 The protonmotive potential

In his original theory of chemiosmosis, Mitchell suggested that energy was stored entirely as a gradient of protons across the mitochondrial inner membrane. However, this membrane is impermeable to all ions, so the ionic composition in the matrix can be quite different from that in the cytosol. Transport of ions would lead to the development of an electrical potential across the membrane in addition to a proton gradient. Therefore, protons would be driven back into the matrix by the proton gradient itself as well as the electrical pressure from the potential difference (ψ) across the membrane. The combination of these two, which he termed the protonmotive potential (Δ_p), is equal to

$$\Delta_p = \psi - 2.303 \, RT/F\Delta\mathrm{pH}$$

where R is the universal gas constant, T is the absolute temperature, F is the Faraday constant and Δ_{pH} the proton gradient across the membrane.

3.5 Stoichiometry of the process

Since the inner membrane of the mitochondrion is impermeable to protons, there should be a strict stoichiometry between the number of protons transported through the ATP synthase and the amount of ATP synthesized (Mitchell, 1966). Experimentally, this number is very difficult to measure and there are still disagreements about it. Mitchell originally suggested that the ratio was 2, but more recent estimates indicate that it could be as high as 3.

Similarly, there should be a strict stoichiometry between the number of electrons transported down the electron transport chain and the number of protons ejected from the matrix. Again this ratio is difficult to measure, but a value of 6 was originally proposed by Mitchell. This would allow three ATP molecules to be synthesized for every two electrons passing through the entire chain. He suggested that there were three sites of proton transport, each one transporting two protons. However, more recent measurements have suggested that each site actually transports four protons, the excess being used for the transport of ions into the matrix.

3.6 The coupling of ATP synthesis to electron transport

In intact mitochondria, electron flow is coupled to ATP synthesis so that the electron-transport chain does not operate when ATP cannot be synthesized as, for example, when ADP and phosphate are not available. One of the most powerful arguments in favour of the chemiosmotic theory is that the two processes can be uncoupled. This allows electron flow to occur without ATP being synthesized. This situation is induced when chemicals, called uncoupling agents, are added to mitochondria. These agents, such as 2,4-dinitrophenol, dissolve in the membrane and facilitate the transport of protons across the membrane. In their presence, a gradient never develops since it is constantly discharged by the uncoupling agent. This demonstrates the requirement for a proton gradient in ATP synthesis and is consistent with the chemiosmotic scheme.

The chemiosmotic theory also explains the mechanism by which ATP synthesis is coupled to electron transport. The electron-transport chain operates to generate a proton gradient. However, in the absence of ATP synthesis the gradient will not be discharged and will become so large that it will exceed the capacity of the chain to pump protons against the back pressure it exerts. When ATP synthesis commences the gradient will be discharged and the passage of electrons down the chain will again be initiated.

3.7 Experimental evidence in favour of chemiosmosis

The first evidence in favour of Mitchell's scheme came from work not on mitochondria but on chloroplasts (see Dennis (1983)). In the light, chloroplasts transport protons from the medium into the thylakoids. This transport of protons is associated with the synthesis of ATP. This was shown by illuminating chloroplasts in the absence of ADP and phosphate, and then adding these when the chloroplasts had been placed in the dark. It was found that the chloroplasts retained their ability to synthesize ATP for a short period of time in the dark. This was originally thought to be due to an energized state of the chloroplasts and was termed X_E. With the advent of chemiosmosis, it was realized that X_E was in fact a proton gradient that persisted after illumination for a short period of time.

In an elegant series of experiments, Jagendorf and his coworkers demonstrated that chloroplasts could synthesize ATP entirely in the dark when a pH gradient was artificially imposed over the thylakoid membranes. The inner space of the thylakoids can be loaded with protons by placing the membranes in an acid medium. On subsequent transfer to an alkaline solution a pH gradient can be formed across the membrane. If ADP and phosphate are then added to the chloroplasts, ATP is synthesized. Hence, the sole function of light in ATP synthesis in chloroplasts is the generation of a proton gradient. This gradient is subsequently used by a chloroplast ATP synthase to form ATP in a process that does not require light. It will operate even when an artificial gradient is imposed across the membrane. This type of experiment, known as the 'Jagendorf jump', has been used to synthesize ATP not only in chloroplasts but also, more recently, in mitochondria.

CHAPTER FOUR

THE ELECTRON-TRANSPORT CHAIN
IN MITOCHONDRIA

4.1 Introduction

The electron-transport chain in plant mitochondria has not been studied as extensively as that in animals. Therefore, although the following account will deal primarily with plants, much of the background is derived from the research on animal mitochondria. It must, however, be realized that even though animals and plants have many features in common, they are by no means identical, since many aspects of plant metabolism are quite different from those found in animals.

4.2 The number of components in the chain

One observation that has not yet been resolved is that the mitochondrial electron-transport chain contains a large number of components; a conservative estimate is that there are at least 21 in animals. The chain is obviously complex, and this complexity is almost certainly essential. What are the possible functions for so many compounds in the chain?

Not all electron-transfer components can react together, so some may be present simply to facilitate exchange between the components. However, another more fundamental function may be to buffer the electron flow through the chain. Although we can use the concept of redox potential to indicate the affinity of the various compounds for electrons, it is rather meaningless when one considers a single component of a membrane that can be either oxidized or reduced. In theory, each component should go from infinitely positive to infinitely negative potential. This would obviously not allow an orderly flow of electrons down the chain. Also, the oxidation–reduction reactions involved in proton transport across the membrane must release a specific amount of energy. This is required to

27

build up a proton gradient of sufficient magnitude to reverse the unfavourable equilibrium of the ATP synthase reaction when these protons re-enter the mitochondrion during ATP synthesis. It is difficult to see how this could be achieved if the components of the chain were either fully oxidized or fully reduced. However, if instead there were a series of compounds with similar redox potentials and between which electrons could rapidly interchange, then there would be a pool of electrons at one potential. The addition to or removal of one electron from the pool would not affect the potential of the pool significantly, and distinct potential drops between the pools could be maintained. This has been termed *redox ballast* (Chance, 1977). What is the magnitude of the potential change that is required for ATP synthesis?

4.3 The potential difference required for ATP synthesis

The standard redox potential change for the oxidation of NADH by oxygen is 1.14 V, which is equivalent to a free energy change of -220 kJ/mol of NADH oxidized. The standard free energy of hydrolysis of ATP is 31 kJ/mol. It is known that there are three coupling sites for ATP synthesis in the electron-transport chain, so in theory it appears that a large amount of energy is wasted when ATP is synthesized. However, it must be realized that, in the mitochondrion, the NAD^+/NADH couple is kept at least 90% oxidized. This means that the actual free energy available is probably nearer 170 kJ/mol of NADH oxidized. In addition, the ATP/ADP ratio is at least 10:1, and values for the actual rather than the standard free energy change required for ATP synthesis have been calculated to be possibly as high as 50 kJ/mol. From considerations such as these, efficiencies of energy transduction have been calculated and high or low values have been presented. However, such calculations are essentially meaningless. High efficiencies are obtained only for reactions operating near equilibrium. As indicated earlier, most pathways in cells are far from equilibrium and much of the energy has to be expended to maintain these unfavourable equilibria.

From the calculations of the free energy required for ATP synthesis under the conditions found in the mitochondrion, it has been estimated that something of the order of 250 mV of electrical potential difference is required at each coupling site in the chain where protons are transported out of the mitochondrion. In theory, it should be possible to operate the chain with only three components, each one catalysing a reaction with a free energy change of 250 mV coupled to a site of ATP synthesis. However, with only three components in the chain it would be difficult to achieve stable redox drops of this magnitude. As described above, the presence of redox pools may stabilize these redox drops at sites of proton pumping.

4.4 The composition of the chain

In animal mitochondria, the electron-transport chain has been separated into four complexes, each catalysing a particular reaction in the chain and three of them being directly involved in ATP synthesis (Figure 4.1). A similar resolution of the chain in plants has not so far been described in as much detail, but from what is known, it is highly likely that complexes similar to those in animals exist. The four complexes catalyse the following reactions:

Complex I. NADH: ubiquinone oxidoreductase

$$NADH + UQ + H^+ \leftrightarrow NAD^+ + UQH_2$$

Complex II. Succinate: ubiquinone oxidoreductase

$$succinate + UQ \leftrightarrow fumarate + UQH_2$$

Complex III. Dihydroquinone: cytochrome c oxidoreductase

$$UQH_2 + 2\,ferricytochrome\,c \leftrightarrow UQ + 2\,ferrocytochrome\,c + 2H^+$$

Complex IV. Cytochrome c: oxygen oxidoreductase (cytochrome oxidase)

$$4\,ferrocytochrome\,c + 4H^+ + O_2 \leftrightarrow 4\,ferricytochrome\,c + 2H_2O$$

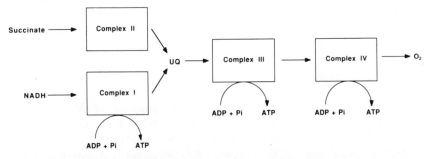

Figure 4.1 A schematic representation of the four complexes of the electron transport chain in animal mitochondria. The three coupling sites, that is, sites where protons are transported out of the mitochondrion, are indicated by the formation of ATP from ADP and phosphate (Pi).

These complexes occur in a 1:1:1:1 ratio and, although they are normally drawn in a linear chain, it must be remembered that they are in fact part of a fluid lipid bilayer and are mobile in the inner membrane.

The individual complexes can be isolated and shown to catalyse each reaction. They can also be combined so that segments of the chain can be catalysed. If all components are added together in the correct ratio, the complete chain from NADH to oxygen can be reconstituted.

Electrons are transferred between the complexes of the membrane by mobile carriers dissolved in the lipid phase of the membrane that can shuttle electrons between them. In plants, there are more complexes than are found in animal mitochondria and the mobile carriers may have a special importance in regulating the flow of electrons into the various complexes.

For further details, see Dennis (1983), Douce (1985), Hatefi (1985), Moore and Rich (1980, 1985), Storey (1980).

4.5 The mobile carriers

4.5.1 Ubiquinone

Ubiquinone is lipid soluble and acts as a mobile carrier between the first three complexes of the electron-transport chain. Ubiquinone in plants is identical with that found in animals and consists of a quinone ring system to which is attached an isoprene chain of ten residues. In plants, ubiquinone plays a central role as it serves to accept electrons, not only from the complexes of the main chain described below but also from the complexes unique to plants. It appears to function as a control point and may determine the path the electrons take at any one time.

4.5.2 Cytochrome c

Cytochrome c is also a mobile carrier acting between Complexes III and IV in the chain. Cytochrome c is readily extracted from mitochondria and is loosely bound to the external surface of the inner membrane. Although there is considerable variation between the structures of cytochrome c from different species, there appears to be a conservation of the active site of the molecule as cytochrome c can be interchanged between the different species and even between plants and animals.

4.6 The complexes of the chain

4.6.1 The reactions of Complex I

Complex I catalyses the transfer of electrons from NADH to ubiquinone (UQ)—see Dennis (1983), Palmer and Ward (1985), Storey (1980). It contains, in both plants and animals, two distinct types of components. In animals there is one molecule of FMN that accepts electrons from the NADH generated in the matrix of the mitochondrion. This part of the complex must, therefore, protrude into the matrix. Also associated with the complex are approximately six iron–sulphur centres. The structure in plants appears to be similar, although it is not clear that the flavoprotein is FMN. Exactly how the complex is arranged in plants is not known. The principal difference between flavoproteins and iron–sulphur centres is that the former transports two hydrogen atoms (i.e. equivalent to two protons plus two electrons) whereas the latter transports only electrons. This is important in mechanisms of energy transduction and will be discussed later. Complex I is involved in transporting protons out of the matrix of the mitochondrion.

4.6.2 The reactions of Complex II

Complex II catalyses the transfer of electrons from succinate to ubiquinone with the reduction of ubiquinone to the dihydroquinone and the formation of fumarate. Proton transfer is not associated with this complex. The animal complex contains one molecule of FAD that is covalently bound into the complex. It also contains three iron–sulphur centres. The FAD reacts directly with succinate in the matrix. It is assumed that the iron–sulphur centres are involved in the transfer of electrons from the FAD to the ubiquinone that is dissolved in the membrane. The plant complex has not been studied to the same extent, but it is generally accepted that it contains a flavoprotein and there is good evidence for the same or similar iron–sulphur centres. In animals, and probably in plants, the complex is regulated. When oxaloacetic acid is bound to the enzyme, the complex is inactive. The presence of increased concentrations of oxaloacetic acid would indicate that the tricarboxylic acid cycle is not active. The bound inhibitor can be removed by the addition of various metabolites such as succinate and phosphate. For further details see Dennis (1983), Douce (1985), Storey (1980).

4.6.3 The reactions of Complex III

Complex III catalyses the transfer of electrons from dihydroubiquinone to cytochrome c, and in the process protons are transported out of the mitochondrion. In animals, it is clear that there are two molecules of cytochrome b in the complex and these appear to be involved in the acceptance of electrons from ubiquinone. The exact location of these molecules in the membrane has not been resolved, but there is evidence that they are placed asymmetrically across the membrane. On isolation, the two molecules are identical and must, therefore, assume their different properties through their interaction with the membrane. Also associated with the complex is one molecule of cytochrome c_1. This is orientated in the membrane such that it can interact with cytochrome c itself on the cytosolic side of the inner membrane. In animals, but not in plants, there is one iron–sulphur centre associated with the complex, often called the Rieske centre after the researcher who first described it. The function of this centre is not known.

A large amount of effort has been expended in trying to elucidate the nature of this complex in plants—so far with only limited success. The complex is clearly different from that in animals. It contains at least two and possibly three cytochrome b molecules and one molecule of cytochrome c_1, but apparently no iron–sulphur centre. Instead, a flavoprotein has been detected and it has been suggested that it is this molecule that is involved in the acceptance of electrons from dihydroubiquinone. The difference in the nature of the plant complex, compared to that found in animals, may be a result of the differences in the function of the electron transport chain between plants and animals. This will be discussed later. (See Dennis (1983), Douce (1985), Rieske (1976), Storey (1980).)

4.6.4 The reactions of Complex IV

Complex IV catalyses the transfer of electrons from cytochrome c to oxygen. It is the third site of proton transfer in the electron-transport chain. Complex IV contains two cytochrome a molecules which, although they can be distinguished in the mitochondrion, appear to be identical on extraction. Associated with each of the cytochrome a molecules is a copper atom, so there are two pairs of electron carriers each of which can transfer two electrons. The first pair, the cytochrome $a–Cu_A$ pair accepts electrons from cytochrome c on the cytosolic side of the membrane. The other pair, cytochrome $a_3–Cu_B$, binds oxygen and is involved in its reduction to water. This reduction requires four electrons, and it has been suggested that the cytochrome a_3–Cu_B pair donates two electrons to the oxygen. This pair is then immediately reduced by the cytochrome a–Cu_B pair and two more electrons are passed on to the oxygen to complete the reduction. The cytochrome a–Cu_A pair, therefore, acts as a reserve of two electrons so that four electrons can be rapidly passed to the oxygen to prevent the build-up of toxic intermediates.

In plants, the complex has not been described in the same amount of detail. All the evidence suggests that it is similar to that described in animals. The properties of the cytochromes and the number of proteins constituting the complex seem to be the same as those in animals, so it can be assumed to operate in a similar fashion. See Dennis (1983), Douce (1985), Storey (1980).

4.7 Other complexes in plant mitochondria

4.7.1 Introduction

Plants differ from animals in having other complexes as part of the electron-transport chain, which confer properties on plants that are not found in animals but which are essential to the function of the plant. Plant mitochondria are much more involved with biosynthetic activity than are animal mitochondria, and hence must be able to exchange material and catalyse reactions that are not seen in animal mitochondria. They must also have more flexibility in their ability to oxidize reducing equivalents that are produced during the various biosynthetic activities. In leaves, mitochondria are an essential component of the photorespiratory pathway which may account for the largest component of mitochondrial metabolism in the light. A schematic arrangement of the complexes in plant mitochondria is shown in Figure 4.2.

4.7.2 The external NADH dehydrogenase

Plant mitochondria, in contrast with those in animals, can oxidize cytosolic NADH. Originally this was thought to be due to the difficulty of isolating the organelle intact. However, it is now accepted that plants have a complex located on the outer surface of the inner membrane that can interact with NADH from the cytosol. It must be remembered, of course, that the outer membrane of the mitochondrion is permeable to molecules of molecular

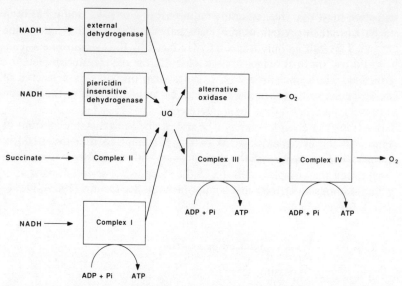

Figure 4.2 A schematic representation of the electron transport chain as it might possibly occur in plant mitochondria. The coupling sites for proton transport are indicated. The central role of ubiquinone is evident in this diagram.

weight up to 10 000, so that there is no barrier to the NADH reaching the inner membrane.

The external dehydrogenase donates electrons to ubiquinone and hence bypasses the first site of proton transport in Complex I. Hence, only two molecules of ATP are synthesized for every two electrons that pass down the chain. The mechanism by which this dehydrogenase is regulated is not known. Calcium may be involved, and may serve to reduce the negative charge on the surface of the membrane. This charge may inhibit the interaction of NADH with the membrane.

For reviews see Dennis (1983), Douce (1985), Moore and Rich (1985), Palmer and Ward (1985), Storey (1980).

4.7.3 The alternative internal NADH dehydrogenase

Plant mitochondria are heavily involved in biosynthetic activities, and may at times have to oxidize substrates even when ATP concentrations are high. It has been suggested that plants possess a second internal NADH dehydrogenase that bypasses the proton pumping site in Complex I. Some NADH-producing reactions may feed electrons directly into this complex, or it may be utilized only when ATP levels are high. This second complex was shown to exist when it was found that the oxidation of some metabolites was not affected by piericidin, an inhibitor that specifically inhibits Complex I by binding to the iron–sulphur centres. See Dennis (1983), Douce (1985), Moore and Rich (1985), Palmer and Ward (1985), Storey (1980).

4.7.4 The alternative oxidase

It has been found that in some cases the electron flow through the electron-transport chain of plant mitochondria is not reduced when inhibitors of the electron-transport chain that act on Complexes III or IV are added to the mitochondrion. This pathway is due to an alternative oxidase that takes electrons from ubiquinone and passes them directly to oxygen, hence bypassing Complexes III and IV. This pathway is now usually called the *alternative pathway*, but may also be called the cyanide-insensitive pathway since it is usually measured by adding cyanide to the organelle or intact tissue and measuring the flow of electrons to oxygen. For a review see Day *et al.* (1980), Dennis (1983), Douce (1985), Lambers (1985), Lance *et al.* (1985), Moore and Rich (1985), Solomos (1977), Storey (1980).

The function of the pathway in most plant tissues is not clear. In the arum lily or skunk cabbage (Meeuse, 1975) it is used to generate heat which volatilizes various perfumes for insect attraction. In other tissues the ratio of this pathway to the normal transport chain is highly variable and can change rapidly, indicating a possible role in normal metabolism. It has been suggested that the alternative oxidase is involved in fruit ripening and seed germination. In these instances, and at other times when there is a high biosynthetic activity, the alternative oxidase may, in conjunction with the external NADH dehydrogenase, serve to oxidize NADH even in the presence of high concentrations of ATP and allow the glycolytic pathway and tricarboxylic acid cycle to operate without inhibition by the accumulation of NADH.

The branch point into the alternative oxidase from the main chain is at ubiquinone. So far no direct control over the flux into this oxidase has been found. It is probable that the alternative pathway acts only as an overflow for the main pathway and comes into operation when the main pathway, as indicated by the redox state of ubiquinone, is highly reduced. In order for this to be effective the standard redox potential of the first component of the alternative oxidase would need to be significantly more positive than ubiquinone. A flavoprotein with a redox potential that is 50 mV more positive than ubiquinone has been detected in the mitochondrion, and this may be the compound that serves as the electron acceptor for the alternative pathway.

Since the branch point into the alternative oxidase occurs at ubiquinone, the final two sites of proton transport are bypassed and hence no ATP is synthesized. Hence, if electrons are fed into ubiquinone from Complex I and then into the alternative oxidase, only one proton-translocating site is operative and only one ATP molecule is formed as two electrons traverse the chain from NADH to oxygen. If the electrons are derived from the external NADH dehydrogenase or the internal NADH dehydrogenase that bypass Site I, then no ATP is synthesized. Except for one or two exceptions, the alternative oxidase is unique to plants. This is probably a reflection of the importance of biosynthetic activity in plant metabolism, where the concentrations of ATP and reducing power must be kept balanced under all conditions.

4.8 Inhibitors of the electron-transport chain

Much of our knowledge of the electron-transport chain in plants and in animals has resulted from a study of inhibitors of electron transport. Many of these are known, and the use of inhibitors has allowed the sequence of components to be determined (Douce, 1985). There are a number of inhibitors of Complex I which appear to act on the iron–sulphur centres of the complex. The best known of these is rotenone. Also acting at this site is the antibiotic piericidin, which is the most powerful inhibitor. A barbiturate drug, amytal, is also an inhibitor of the iron–sulphur centres. Antimycin A is an inhibitor of b cytochromes, and hence will prevent electron flow through Complex III. There are a number of inhibitors of Complex IV which bind to the oxygen binding site associated with the cytochrome a_3. The best known of these is cyanide. Carbon monoxide also binds to this site, as does azide.

There are specific inhibitors of the alternative pathway that have been used to determine the interaction of this pathway with the main chain. The first inhibitors used for this were substituted hydroxamic acids. These chelate ferric ions, and it was inferred from this that ferric ions were involved in the alternative oxidase, although this is now not thought to be the case. A more potent inhibitor is disulfiram, which may act at a separate site from the hydroxamic acids.

4.9 The mechanism of proton transport in the mitochondrion

4.9.1 Redox loops

There are two types of transport molecule in the electron-transport chain of the inner membrane of the mitochondrion; those that transport electrons, such as the cytochromes and the iron–sulphur centres, and those that transport hydrogens, such as FMN and ubiquinone. In his original theory, Mitchell (1961, 1966) proposed that these are arranged in a vectorial manner across the inner membrane so that electrons are transported in one direction while hydrogens are transported in the opposite sense (Figure 4.3). When a hydrogen carrier is reduced it must accept not only electrons but also protons. If a hydrogen carrier accepts two electrons from the matrix side of the inner membrane, then it must also absorb two protons from the matrix. If the oxidation of the carrier occurs on the cytosolic side then two protons will be released to the cytosol. Hence during the transport of two electrons by the carrier, two protons will be moved across the membrane.

Mitchell suggested that Site I of proton transport (or indirectly of ATP synthesis) occurs in Complex I, where FMN accepts electrons from NADH on the matrix side of the inner membrane and in the process also gains two protons from the matrix. He proposed that the FMN molecule traverses the membrane allowing its oxidation to occur on the cytosolic side. Hence,

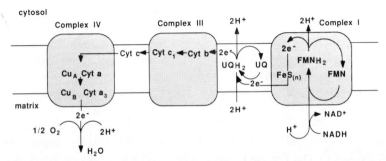

Figure 4.3   The orientation of electron transfer components in the electron transport chain that would result in the transport of protons by a redox loop mechanism as proposed by Mitchell (1961), (1966), (1972), (1976), (1977).

on oxidation protons are extruded into the cytosol. The electrons from the FMN are accepted by the electron-carrying iron–sulphur centres which in turn cross the membrane carrying the electrons back to the matrix side where they are donated to ubiquinone.

Site II of proton transport is formed by ubiquinone, which is soluble and mobile in the membrane. This molecule is reduced on the matrix side by electrons from the iron–sulphur centres of Complex I and in the process takes up two protons from the matrix. Ubiquinone is oxidized by the cytochrome *b* of Complex III, an electron carrier on the cytosolic side, and again releases two protons to the cytosol.

This scheme accounts for the first two sites of proton transport as described by Mitchell. The third site did not involve actual transport of protons. When a molecule of oxygen is reduced it requires not only four electrons but also four protons. The function of Complex IV was thought to be to transport electrons across the inner membrane from Complex III to the matrix where they combine with oxygen to form water; in the process protons are removed from the matrix. The removal of protons from the matrix is equivalent to the transport of protons across the membrane.

4.9.2 The protonmotive Q cycle

It soon became apparent that more protons are required to be transported than are provided by the original redox loop scheme. Mitchell, therefore, modified the redox loop at coupling Site II so that two protons could be transported for each electron that passed through that site. This was accomplished by what was referred to as the protonmotive Q cycle. In this process one electron is cycled back through Complex III to the matrix side of the membrane after the oxidation of ubiquinone while the other continues down the chain to Complex IV. Hence, ubiquinone on the matrix side is reduced by one electron from Complex I and one from Complex III (Figure 4.4). One electron simply cycles round Complex III. The result of the Q cycle is that two protons are transported for every electron traversing this section of the chain.

The introduction of the Q cycle improved the stoichiometry of the proton transport by the inner membrane so that it now conformed to Mitchell's scheme for chemiosmotic coupling. However, other workers suggested that more than two protons were required at each proton transport site since a proton gradient is required, not only for ATP synthesis, but also for the transport of essential ions such as phosphate which is moved into the matrix with the co-transport of a proton. It was

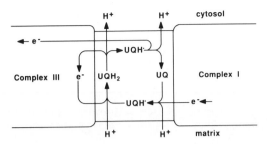

Figure 4.4   A formulation of the protonmotive Q cycle involving complexes I and III and the mobile ubiquinone. In this mechanism two protons are translocated across the membrane for every electron that moves through the electron transport chain. Based on the work of Mitchell (1972), (1976), (1977).

also suggested that the ATP synthase required more than two protons, as had been assumed by Mitchell. All this led to the suggestion that, in addition to the redox loops, proton pumps were directly involved in moving protons across the membrane.

For reviews see Dennis (1983), Douce (1985), Nicholls (1982).

4.9.3 Proton pumps

Pumps for transporting ions of various types are known for all the membranes of the cell, so a pump for proton transport would not be exceptional. The ATP synthase itself will transport protons if it is incorporated into a membrane and then supplied with ATP. Papa (1976) suggested that the electron-transport chain contained proton pumps that moved protons across the membrane as electrons flowed through them. A pump would be associated with each complex involved in energy transduction. This could be in addition to the vectorial transport suggested by Mitchell.

When Complex I is isolated and incorporated into lipid vesicles it will exhibit proton translocation with four protons being translocated for every two electrons passing through it, suggesting that a proton pump is operating in addition to a redox loop. A similar stoichiometry has been reported for Complex III, indicating that a pump is also operative here. Complex IV also appears to be a pump, so that protons are actually moved across the membrane in addition to being removed by oxygen reduction. Overall, therefore, four protons are probably transported at each coupling site. The exact mechanism by which a proton pump operates is not yet known, although several proposals have been made.

The above concepts of proton translocation have been elucidated from work on animal mitochondria. Very little is known about energy transduction in plant mitochondria. It is known that plant mitochondria will develop a proton gradient during electron transport. There is also evidence for the operation of a protonmotive Q cycle in plants. However, since the components of the electron-transport chain are not identical between plants and animals, some differences in the process are likely to emerge. For a review see Dennis (1983). Fillingame (1980), Papa (1976), Wikstrom *et al.* (1981).

4.10 ATP synthesis in the mitochondrion

4.10.1 The structure of the ATP synthase

The ATP synthase is a complex of at least 12 proteins that can be resolved into two distinct groups; the membrane-associated complex or F_0 and the matrix-associated portion or F_1 (see Baird and Hames (1979), Cross (1981), Dennis (1983) and Hatefi (1985)). The F_1 portion protrudes into the mitochondrion and can be visualized by electron microscopy. These two parts are joined together by a stalk composed of two proteins. The F_1 portion of the molecule can easily be isolated and has been shown to be made up of five different proteins in animals and probably also in plants. The two largest proteins are present in a $\alpha_2\beta_2$ stoichiometry. The active site of the complex is most likely on the β subunit, although the α subunit may also be required for its formation. The α subunit also binds nucleotides and may be involved in the regulation of the complex. On isolation, F_1 will hydrolyse ATP; this is latent in the mitochondrion, probably due to one of the proteins acting as an inhibitor. The main function of the other subunits in F_1 may be to bind the complex to the stalk.

The F_0 complex is incorporated into, and spans, the membrane as an integral protein complex. F_0 consists of three proteins one of which, the proteolipid, forms a channel in the membrane that will allow the passage of protons. The function of the other two proteins is as yet unknown. When F_1 is separated from F_0, the inner membrane of the mitochondrion becomes leaky to protons. This can be rectified by binding F_1 back onto the F_0. The channel can also be blocked by inhibitors of oxidative phosphorylation such as DCCD that binds to the proteolipid of F_0.

The F_1 of the complex is attached to the membrane by two proteins. One of these has been termed the oligomycin sensitivity conferring protein

(OSCP). Oligomycin is another inhibitor of oxidative phosphorylation. It will also inhibit the ATPase activity of the F_1, but only when the F_1 is attached to F_0 through the OSCP. It appears that the binding site for oligomycin is on F_0, so that the inhibitory effect of oligomycin must be transmitted to F_1 via a conformational change through the OSCP. The complex undoubtedly undergoes a series of conformational changes that may be important in oxidative phosphorylation, as will be described below.

4.10.2 The formation of ATP

The detailed mechanism by which the energy that is stored as a proton gradient is used to synthesize ATP on the ATP synthase is unknown. Mitchell has proposed a mechanism whereby a proton from the cytosol is channelled to the active site of the ATP synthase by means of the proton channel in F_0. This proton could be forced, because of the proton gradient, into close contact with an oxygen of a phosphate bound to the active site of the synthase which would alter the properties of the phosphate and make it more reactive towards ADP.

A second distinct mechanism has been proposed by Boyer (1977a, b). The equilibrium position of the ATP synthase reaction is normally accepted to lie very much in favour of ATP hydrolysis. However, it must be remembered that this is only under normal cellular conditions. Under acidic or hydrophobic conditions the reaction is reversible, and may even favour ATP synthesis. Boyer proposed that on the binding of ADP and

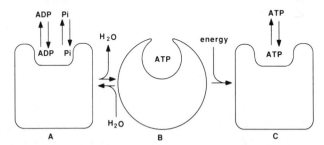

Figure 4.5 A conformational mechanism for the formation of ATP. In the first reaction ADP and phosphate are enclosed, through a conformational change, in a hydrophobic region of the ATP synthase, water is eliminated and ATP formed. However, in order for the ATP to be liberated from the active site of the enzyme energy must be supplied, probably involving a proton gradient, to cause a conformation change of the protein. The first reaction is readily reversible. In the second reaction uncouplers prevent energy being supplied to the ATP synthase and hence, the conformation change is inhibited and the release of the ATP prevented. From the work of Boyer (1977 a, b), adapted from Dennis (1983).

phosphate to the active site of the ATP synthase, a conformational change takes place that encloses the substrates in a hydrophobic region of the enzyme. The conditions encountered in this region may be quite different from those found in the cytosol or matrix of the mitochondrion, and may in fact favour ATP synthesis. Hence, ATP may be formed without actually requiring an input of energy. However, this would leave the ATP embedded in the interior of the enzyme. Boyer proposed that energy was required to change the conformation of the enzyme so that ATP could be released (Figure 4.5). This conformational change could be brought about by the passage of protons through the ATP synthase complex. Dinitrophenol would prevent the input of energy in the form of a proton flux that is required for the conformational change. Boyer has modified his original theory to include two active sites that alternate between loose and tight binding. Although it may appear at first sight that ATP is being synthesized without the expenditure of energy, the actual free energy required for ATP synthesis must be the same whatever the mechanism. In the case of Boyer's conformational coupling theory, the energy is used to change the environment at the active site of the ATP synthase from one favouring synthesis to one favouring hydrolysis. Since the latter conditions are the same as those in the cytosol, the ATP can then be released.

4.10.3 Reconstituting ATP synthesis

As mentioned earlier, the main problem in the study of energy transduction has been the requirement for an intact membrane for the system to operate. A major advance was made by Racker and his coworkers (Racker, 1977) when they showed that ATP can be synthesized in a system reconstituted from purified components. The mechanism for generating a proton gradient was developed from the bacterium *Halobacterium halobium*. This bacterium has purple patches in its cellular membrane that on illumination pump protons out of the cell and generate a proton gradient that can be used for ATP synthesis by the bacterium. These purple patches can readily be purified and, when they are incorporated into lipid vesicles made from the phospholipids of the soybean seed, they will, on illumination, transport protons across the membrane and hence develop a gradient. If the F_0 is also incorporated into the vesicles the gradient is discharged through the proton channel. However, if the F_1 is now attached to the F_0 by means of the OSCP then, in the presence of ADP and phosphate, ATP can be synthesized. It is of interest to note that this reconstituted system is made up of components from plants, animals and bacteria.

CHAPTER FIVE

ENERGY TRANSDUCTION IN THE CHLOROPLAST

5.1 Introduction

Energy transduction in the chloroplast is energetically the reverse of that described in the mitochondrion, in that the process involves the reduction of $NAPDP^+$, an analogue of NAD^+, with electrons from water. During this oxidation of water, oxygen and protons are released. In the mitochondrion, energy is released during the oxidation of NADH by oxygen via the electron transport chain. Conversely, energy is required in photosynthesis; this energy is supplied by photons of light energy.

It is necessary in photosynthesis, therefore, to remove electrons from water, a redox couple that has a standard redox potential of $+0.81$ V, and transfer them to the $NADP^+/NAPDH$ couple which has a standard redox potential of -0.32 V. In theory one quantum of red light has sufficient energy to facilitate this transfer. However, as has already been discussed, it is necessary to consider the equilibrium position of the reactions. In order to remove an electron from water effectively a redox potential much more positive than $+0.81$ V has to be developed, or the system would simply go to equilibrium. Similarly, an electron donor with a potential more negative than -0.32 V has to be reduced to transfer electrons to $NADP^+$ effectively. When considerations such as these are included in the calculations it can be shown that a single photon of light energy is insufficient for this electron transfer. Hence, it has been concluded that the energy from two photons is required.

From considerations such as those described above, and also from direct experimental evidence, it has been concluded that there are two light-absorbing photosystems that cooperate in the reduction of $NADP^+$ by electrons derived from water (see Arnon, 1977; Gregory, 1978). This is commonly referred to as the Z scheme, and is shown in Figure 5.1. Both photosystems are embedded in the thylakoid membranes of the chloroplast. The initial event in each photosystem is the absorption of a quantum

43

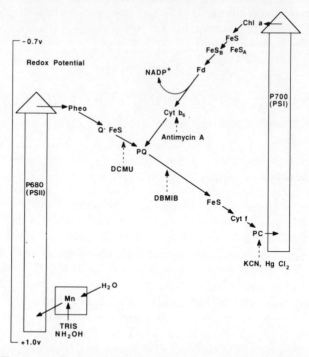

Figure 5.1 The cooperation of two light reactions in the reduction of NADP$^+$ from electrons derived from water. The redox scale gives an indication of the redox potentials developed by the photosystems. Abbreviations used are: PSII, photosystem II; pheo, pheophytin; Q.FeS, bound plastoquinone and an iron–sulphur centre; DCMU, dichloro-phenylmethyl urea; cyt f, cytochrome f; PC, plastocyanin; KCN, potassium cyanide; PSI, photosystem I; Fd, ferredoxin; cyt b_6, cytochrome b_6.

of light energy (a photon). This absorbed energy causes a charge separation across the membrane. The positive charge is directed towards the thylakoid vesicle, and the negative towards the stroma. This charge separation is very unstable and there must be acceptor molecules for these charges that are closely associated with both photosystems. The charges are neutralized by removing an electron from the negatively charged side and donating an electron to the positively charged side. This returns the photosystem to the ground state. An effective transfer requires that there is a large potential difference between the primary reductant and its electron acceptor, and the primary oxidant and its electron donor.

In the Z scheme, Photosystem I produces a strong reductant with a very negative redox potential which is approximately -0.6 V. This reductant donates electrons ultimately to $NADP^+$. However, the oxidant produced by this system has an insufficiently positive redox potential to oxidize water. In contrast, Photosystem II produces a weak reductant but an oxidant that has a potential positive enough effectively to remove electrons from water. An essential feature of the scheme is that the energy input into the two photosystems must be balanced, or a reduction in the efficiency of photosynthesis will result. This can be induced experimentally under certain conditions, and was the original indication that two photosystems were present.

5.2 The primary reactions

The two photosystems are spatially separated in higher plant chloroplasts, Photosystem II being found preferentially in the grana (stacked thylakoid membranes) and Photosystem I in the non-stacked membranes (stromal thylakoids). Associated with each photosystem are light-harvesting molecules. In Photosystem I these consist principally of chlorophyll a molecules, whereas in Photosystem II, in addition to chlorophyll a, chlorophyll b and other accessory pigments are found. The light-harvesting molecules have the function of trapping light energy and funnelling it to the reaction centres of the photosystems. The light-harvesting molecules are associated with proteins to form the light-harvesting complexes. These complexes are not fixed in the membranes, but can migrate.

Normally the light-harvesting complexes are associated with Photosystem II, but under conditions where the energy being received by Photosystem II exceeds that of Photosystem I, the light-harvesting complexes are phosphorylated by an enzyme which causes them to migrate to the area of the membrane containing Photosystem I. This increases the ability of Photosystem I to trap light energy. When Photosystem I is receiving excessive energy the light-harvesting molecules are dephosphorylated and they then migrate back to the grana and associate with Photosystem II. Hence, because of this constant migration of the light-harvesting complexes between the grana and the non-stacked membranes the input of light energy into the two photosystems is balanced (Arntzen, 1978; Junge, 1977; Sane, 1977).

The reaction centre where the actual charge separation occurs is made up of a chlorophyll a molecule, or a dimer of chlorophyll a molecules, closely associated with the light-trapping molecules which in turn interact with the light-harvesting complexes. There are at least 250 light-trapping molecules for every chlorophyll a molecule at the reaction centre. A photosystem, therefore, consists of the reaction centre, molecules for donating and accepting electrons from the reaction centre, and the light-trapping molecules. It must be remembered that every chlorophyll molecule in the membrane is associated with protein molecules and this association alters the properties of the chlorophyll molecule.

The chlorophyll *a* molecules at the reaction centres of the two photosystems, which behave identically to all other chlorophyll *a* molecules on isolation, absorb at longer wavelengths when they are in the membrane. The change in the properties of the chlorophyll is due to its association with chlorophyll-binding proteins. Hence the chlorophyll *a* molecule at the reaction centre of Photosystem I has a maximum absorbance at 700 nm, whereas that at the reaction centre of Photosystem II has a maximum absorbance at 680 nm. This is in contrast to chlorophyll *a* in solution, which has maximum absorbance at 660 nm. Hence, the chlorophyll molecules at the two reaction centres are often referred to as P700 and P680 (P simply meaning pigment).

For reviews, see Cogdell (1983); Dennis (1983); Ke (1978); Mathis and Paillotin (1981).

5.3 The reactions of the photosystems

5.3.1 Introduction

The energetic relationship of the two photosystems is shown in Figure 5.1 and the spatial arrangement in the membrane of the thylakoid in

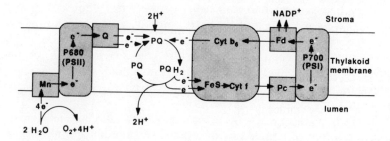

Figure 5.2 The possible mechanism by which a proton gradient is developed across the thylakoid membrane of the chloroplast during noncyclic and cyclic flow of electrons. Non-cyclic flow of electrons involves both Photosystem I and II as electrons are transported from water to $NADP^+$. Cyclic flow involves only Photosystem I. Ferredoxin (Fd) is the branch point in the system feeding electrons either to $NADP^+$ or to the cyclic pathway.

Figure 5.2. It must be realized, however, that this is just a stylized representation and that the two photosystems are in fact separate in the grana and the non-stacked membranes.

5.3.2 Photosystem II

In the photosystem, a photon of light energy absorbed by the accessory pigments or the other chlorophyll molecules is passed to the chlorophyll *a* molecule (P680) at the reaction centre (Cogdell, 1983; Dennis, 1983; Mathis and Paillotin, 1981; Velthuys, 1980). Since P680 absorbs at a longer wavelength than the other chlorophyll molecules the photon is trapped at the reaction centre long enough for a chemical reaction to take place. The chlorophyll molecule on the acceptance of the photon becomes an excited molecule in which an electron is raised into a new orbital. The excited molecule is orientated across the membrane and this causes a charge separation to occur across the membrane with the negative charge on the stromal side of the membrane. In effect the chlorophyll *a* molecule at the reaction centre in the excited state becomes a more effective reducing agent so that it can donate an electron at a potential of around -0.45 V. In this excited state, the electron can be removed from P680 by an acceptor molecule that is probably a pheophytin dimer. Pheophytin has the structure of a chlorophyll molecule but lacks the magnesium atom in the porphyrin ring. This pheophytin molecule is located on the stromal side of the membrane.

The removal of the electron leaves the chlorophyll *a* molecule at the reaction centre with a positive charge. This positive charge is neutralized by the donation of an electron from the water-splitting complex on the lumen side of the membrane. Hence the initial event is the generation of a positive charge on the inside of the membrane and a negative charge on the outside.

The oxidation of water to produce one molecule of oxygen requires the removal of four electrons from two molecules of water (Diner and Joliot, 1977; Mathis and Paillotin, 1981). It appears that the water-splitting complex of Photosystem II has a mechanism for storing oxidizing equivalents until four are available to enable a concerted reaction to occur with the release of a molecule of oxygen. This was originally shown by the fact that when Photosystem II is activated by very short pulses of light, oxygen is evolved only every fourth flash. How these oxidizing equivalents are stored is not known, but it is known that manganese is essential for the water-splitting reaction. Manganese can assume a number of oxidation states, which would ideally suit it for this role. The manganese is attached to a protein on the inner surface of the thylakoid membrane. Hence, the oxidation of water results in the liberation of oxygen into the lumen of the thylakoid but, more importantly, also in the release of four protons for every oxygen molecule produced. These protons contribute to the formation of a proton gradient across the membrane.

The ultimate electron acceptor of Photosystem II is plastoquinone. This has a structure and function very similar to the ubiquinone in the mitochondrion (Amesz, 1977). It is mobile in the thylakoid membrane and is a hydrogen carrier. In the process of being reduced and oxidized it transports protons across the membrane and hence contributes to the proton gradient. Plastoquinone cannot interact directly with the reaction centre of the photosystem. There are, therefore, a series of molecules that facilitate this transfer.

Closely associated with the photosystem itself is a pheophytin molecule with a fairly negative redox potential of around -0.45 V. This passes the electrons on to what is probably a bound plastoquinone molecule that may be associated with an iron–sulphur centre. One problem that has to be overcome is that the reaction centre is a single-electron donor, whereas plastoquinone carries two electrons. The arrangement of the bound plastoquinone with an iron–sulphur centre may be a means of converting a single-electron flow into a two-electron transfer.

The removal of the excited electron from the P680 must be very effective, or else the trapped energy is lost. This loss occurs by the excited electron in P680 falling back to the ground state and in the process emitting a photon with a wavelength very similar to that of the photon in the exciting light. This fluorescence can only be detected in chloroplasts when the electron acceptors, such as plastoquinone, are highly reduced and cannot accept the electron from the excited P680. This can occur, for example, when the electron-transport chain becomes the rate-limiting step in the entire process and blocks the flow of electrons from the reaction centre of the photosystem. The measurement of the fluorescence of P680 was the principal means by which the nature of the acceptor molecules in Photosystem II was studied for many years. Some herbicides such as dichlorophenylmethyl urea (DCMU) interact with the components between Photosystem I and plastoquinone, preventing the transfer of electrons from P680. This causes the acceptor molecules in the photosystem to become reduced and in turn enhances the fluorescence of P680.

In summary, Photosystem II produces a strong oxidant that is capable of oxidizing water, the oxidizing equivalents being stored until two molecules of water can be oxidized to a molecule of oxygen with the release of four protons into the lumen of the thylakoid. The photosystem also produces a reductant of approximately -0.450 V, which rapidly loses an electron to an acceptor and ultimately to plastoquinone. Plastoquinone has a redox potential of 0 V, so there is a loss of energy on the reduction of this component which traps the electron from the photosystem and prevents the loss of energy by fluorescence. However, when plastoquinone becomes highly reduced, the transfer of electrons from the primary acceptors is inhibited and the fluorescence can then be seen and measured.

5.3.3 Photosystem I

The ultimate electron acceptor for Photosystem I is ferredoxin, a small iron–sulphur protein that is loosely associated with the stromal surface of the thylakoid membrane (Hall and Rao, 1977). Ferredoxin distributes electrons to various acceptors and hence represents a branch point in electron flow in photosynthesis. As was the case with plastoquinone in Photosystem II, ferredoxin cannot interact directly with the reaction centre, P700, of the photosystem and hence there must be intermediate carriers of which at least four have been reported.

The immediate electron acceptor from the excited P700 appears to be a chlorophyll *a* molecule or dimer. This, in turn, donates the electron to an iron–sulphur centre which then transfers it to a pair of iron–sulphur centres termed Centres A and B. These centres have a redox potential that is more negative than -0.55 V, so the potential developed by the reaction centre itself must be even more negative than this. Hence, as was the case in the other photosystem, there is a complex for transferring electrons from the reaction centre of the photosystem to a component that is loosely bound to the centre.

The immediate electron donor to Photosystem I is plastocyanin, a small copper-containing protein (Katoh, 1977). There are approximately 10 plastocyanin molecules to every P700 reaction centre. Some of the plastocyanin is tightly bound to the reaction centre complex, although most of it is loosely bound and can easily be removed by sonication. This loosely bound plastocyanin probably acts as a mobile carrier in the membrane in a similar way to the role played by cytochrome *c* in the mitochondrial electron-transport chain. The standard redox potential of plastocyanin is $+0.350$ V.

Photosystem I, therefore, produces a powerful reductant with a potential of at least -0.600 V and an oxidant with a potential low enough to accept electrons from plastocyanin; that is, it must have a potential that is more positive than $+0.35$ V. Once again the function of the electron acceptors in the photosystem is to remove an electron from P700 rapidly enough to prevent the excitation energy being lost as fluorescence.

For further details see Cogdell (1983), Dennis (1983), Ke (1978), Malkin (1982), Malkin and Bearden (1978), Mathis and Paillotin (1981).

5.4 The photosynthetic electron transport chain

5.4.1 The components of the chain

The two photosystems are connected by an electron-transport chain that takes electrons from plastoquinone at a midpoint potential of 0 V to plastocyanin with a midpoint potential of $+0.35$ V. (See Avron (1981), Cramer and Whitmarsh (1977), Goldbeck et al (1977), Haehnel (1984), Velthuys (1980).) Sufficient energy is released as electrons are transferred from plastoquinone to plastocyanin for this to be a site of proton pumping across the membrane from the stroma into the lumen of the thylakoid. This ultimately results in the synthesis of ATP. The components of the electron-transport chain can be isolated as a complex that in many ways resembles Complex III of the mitochondrion. It contains an iron–sulphur centre, a c-type cytochrome and a b-type cytochrome. Similarly, the complex accepts electrons from the mobile carrier plastoquinone, an analogue of ubiquinone and passes them on to a second mobile carrier, plastocyanin.

5.4.2 Non-cyclic electron transport

In non-cyclic electron transport electrons are passed from water via the electron-transport chain to ferredoxin and finally to $NADP^+$. Hence, the ultimate electron acceptor is $NADP^+$ which is reduced to NADPH. NADPH is then used in the reactions for the reduction of carbon dioxide to carbohydrate. Both photosystems and the electron-transport chain are involved in non-cyclic electron transport.

The electron-transport chain, which has been isolated as a complex, transfers electrons from the reducing end of Photosystem II to the oxidizing end of Photosystem I. The ultimate electron acceptor of electrons from the reaction centre of Photosystem II is plastoquinone. From this molecule, electrons are transferred to the iron–sulphur centre, which has a potential of 0.29 V. Compounds that inhibit the transfer of electrons from quinones to iron–sulphur centres stop electron flow in chloroplasts, which demonstrates that this transfer is important in vivo.

The role of cytochrome f, the final component of the electron-transfer complex, has been in dispute in the past, but it now appears that it is in the main chain and acts as an intermediate between the iron–sulphur centre and plastocyanin. It has a redox potential of $+0.36$ V, which is very similar to that of plastocyanin, and at one time it had been suggested that they were on parallel pathways. However, mutants of *Chlamydomonas* have been found that lack either cytochrome f or plastocyanin, and in both cases electron flow is inhibited if one of the components is missing. It is, therefore, now accepted that there is the following linear flow of electrons:

plastoquinone → iron–sulphur centre → cytochrome f → plastocyanin

The energy-conserving step is in the transfer of electrons from plasto-quinone to the iron–sulphur centre, which is the rate-limiting point in the chain and is where protons are pumped into the lumen of the thylakoid.

5.4.3 Cyclic electron flow

As will be discussed later, the reduction of one molecule of carbon dioxide to the level of carbohydrate (the basic process of photosynthesis) requires two molecules of NADPH and three of ATP. Hence there is not a 1:1 stoichiometry between the requirements for these two cofactors. In addition, the chloroplast is involved in other biosynthetic reactions so that the requirements for ATP and NADPH may be different. Non-cyclic electron transport imposes a strict 1:1 stoichiometry between the production of ATP and NADPH. Hence, there must be some mechanism by which ATP can be synthesized independently. This is achieved by a cyclic flow of electrons around Photosystem I that does not involve Photosystem II; nor is NADPH synthesized in the process.

The initial component in the pathway appears to be cytochrome b_6 which accepts electrons from ferredoxin and is therefore at a branch point, delivering electrons either to $NADP^+$ or to cytochrome b_6. In turn, cytochrome b_6 passes the electrons to plastoquinone. The remainder of the pathway is identical in both pathways, in that the electrons are then transported to the oxidizing side of P700 by way of the iron–sulphur centre, cytochrome f and plastocyanin. The coupling site of both pathways is between plastoquinone and the iron–sulphur centre. In cyclic flow, electrons are, therefore, passed from the reducing end of Photosystem I to cytochrome b_6, then via plastoquinone and the electron-transport chain to the oxidizing side of the same photosystem. In the process no oxygen is released nor is $NADP^+$ reduced. The pathway is solely for the production of ATP. The rate of flow of electrons round the cyclic system is controlled by the state of reduction of ferredoxin. Hence, cyclic flow does not commence until ferredoxin is highly reduced, which indicates that the $NADP^+$ couple is also highly reduced. It should be mentioned that in some schemes cytochrome b_6 has been assigned functions other than purely cyclic electron flow. There is good evidence that in chloroplasts there is some form of Q cycle. Cytochrome b_6 could also be involved in this Q cycle for non-cyclic flow.

5.5 The establishment of a proton gradient in chloroplasts

There are two sites where protons are accumulated in the lumen of the thylakoid of the chloroplast as shown in Figure 5.2. In the first place protons are liberated through the oxidation of water, which occurs on the lumen side of thylakoid membrane by means of the water-splitting complex. For every two electrons that are transported from water to $NADP^+$, two protons are released.

The second site occurs at the point where plastoquinone is oxidized by the iron–sulphur complex of the electron-transport chain. The reduction of plastoquinone occurs on the stromal side of the membrane by electrons from Photosystem II. Since plastoquinone is a hydrogen carrier, protons are also required and are taken up by the plastoquinone from the stroma. Its oxidation by the electron-transport chain occurs on the lumen side of the membrane, and hence protons are released into the lumen when plastoquinone is oxidized by the iron–sulphur centre which is an electron carrier. This same proton-transporting site is used by the cyclic flow of electrons except that in this case the electrons for the reduction of plastoquinone are supplied by cytochrome b_6 from Photosystem I.

The stoichiometry of proton accumulation in the lumen of the thylakoid, in relation to electron flow, in theory should be four protons for every two electrons transported from water to $NADP^+$; this ratio has been confirmed. There have been reports of higher ratios, and this has been taken as evidence for the operation of a Q cycle involving cytochrome b_6 similar to the Q cycle in the mitochondrion. For further details see Avron (1981), Dennis (1983), Gimmler (1977), Hanska and Trebst (1977), Jagendorf (1977), Junge (1977).

5.6 The synthesis of ATP

5.6.1 *The structure of the chloroplast ATP synthase*

The chloroplast ATP synthase, or coupling factor, has a structure that is very similar to that described for the mitochondrial synthase. (See Baird and Hammes (1979), Dennis (1983), Gimmler (1977), Jagendorf (1977), Shavit (1980), Strotman and Bicket-Sandkotter (1984).) It consists of two parts; the CF_1, that on isolation catalyses ATP hydrolysis, and the CF_0 that is an integral component of the membrane. These two complexes are associated through a stalk that projects the CF_1 into the stroma.

The CF_1 is composed of five different subunits, designated $\alpha,\beta,\gamma,\delta,\varepsilon$. The stoichiometry of these subunits appears to be $\alpha_2,\beta_2,\gamma,\delta,\varepsilon_2$. The active site of the CF_1 is associated with the β subunit although the α subunit may also be involved. The ATPase activity of the isolated CF_1 is very low and it is thought that the complex is naturally inhibited, possibly by the ε subunit. If this is removed by partial hydrolysis with trypsin the ATPase activity can be found. This can also be revealed by the treatment of the complex with strong reducing agents such as dithiothreitol. The other components of the complex are probably involved in binding the CF_1 to the membrane.

When CF_1 is removed the membrane becomes permeable to protons, indicating that CF_0 forms a channel in it. CF_0 contains a proteolipid subunit which, when incorporated in a membrane, renders it permeable to protons. The proton channel is formed by the cooperative action of four to six of these subunits. The proteolipid will bind DCCD, an inhibitor of photophosphorylation. When DCCD is bound to the proteolipid the permeability to protons is lost. The channel formed by the proteolipid is specific for protons; potassium or chloride ions are not transported, even though these are smaller than a hydrated proton. It is possible that the proton channel is anhydrous and that the hydration shell is stripped from the proton as it enters the channel.

The complex must be highly regulated or it will hydrolyse ATP. The proton gradient could also be dissipated by the channel in CF_0. The coupling complex is inactive in the dark but can be activated by a proton gradient or by light. It has been suggested that CF_1 is activated by the removal of the inhibitory subunit ε from the complex. This removal may be brought about by reduction of the ε subunit by electrons from ferredoxin via a secondary reductant called thioredoxin that is involved in the regulation of other chloroplast enzymes.

Although a great deal is known about the structure of the coupling factor, the mechanism by which ATP is synthesized on the enzyme is not understood. Possible mechanisms for the synthesis of ATP by the ATP synthase have been described previously with reference to the mitochondrial enzyme, as has the experimental evidence in favour of the chemiosmotic theory operating in the chloroplast.

CHAPTER SIX

THE GLYCOLYTIC AND PENTOSE PHOSPHATE PATHWAYS

6.1 The organization of plant metabolism

It is assumed by the majority of biochemists that plant metabolism is very similar to that found in animals and bacteria, but we are now beginning to learn that there are many differences between the metabolism of plants and other organisms. One of the obvious differences is that plants photosynthesize, which is not the case with animals and the majority of bacteria. Hence, plants have a whole system of metabolic pathways unique to this activity. However, even in other pathways that might be expected to be similar, there are often profound differences. Why should this be so?

In the first place, plant metabolism is much more complex than animal metabolism. Plants can take simple inorganic nutrients and convert them into all the metabolites they require. In contrast, animals require a complex diet because they cannot manufacture even some of their most essential metabolites such as vitamins and many amino acids. In addition to this, plants manufacture a whole range of complex organic molecules such as alkaloids and flavanoids that are not found in animals or bacteria, and whose function even in plants is largely unknown.

Secondly, a plant cell may have to undergo radical changes in metabolism that may be quite different from those experienced by animals. A plant cannot move to a new environment if conditions become unfavourable. Hence, it may have to endure radical changes in temperature or water balance. The most important change, however, is the transition from light to dark and *vice versa*. This has the effect of altering the supply of nutrients from those provided by the chloroplast to those supplied by the breakdown of storage or transport metabolites. Clearly there must be a difference in the control of metabolism compared with that found in animals or bacteria.

Thirdly, and most importantly, plant cells contain an organelle that is

55

c

not found in other organisms, namely the *plastid*. The most studied group of plastids are, of course, *chloroplasts*. These are plastids that have photosynthesis as their main function, but it must be remembered that this is only one of the functions that is performed by chloroplasts or by other types of plastid.

Plastids come in many shapes and sizes, and perform different functions in the various cells that make up a plant. All plastids are formed from a common precursor termed a *proplastid*. During cell growth the proplastids divide and differentiate into the type of plastid characteristic of that particular cell type. For example, in storage tubers of the potato, proplastids develop into amyloplasts that are mainly involved in starch biosynthesis and storage; when they are mature they are filled with large starch grains. In developing oilseeds, plastids occur as colourless organelles termed leucoplasts that are mainly involved in the synthesis of fatty acids for storage oils. In some flowers, the plastids occur as chromoplasts which give the colour to the flower and in which the principal metabolism is the synthesis of terpenes.

Plastids are present in all plant tissues and are essential to the metabolism of the tissue. A large proportion of all the biosynthetic activity in a plant cell occurs in some type of plastid. For example, fatty acid biosynthesis is confined to plastids, as is the synthesis of the majority of amino acids and terpenes. It must also be remembered that, although a plastid such as a chloroplast may be specialized for one particular function, other synthetic activities are also present.Chloroplasts, for example, are the site of fatty acid syntheses and of many amino acid biosyntheses especially in leaves. The proportions of each activity may, however, vary considerably in each tissue of a plant.

The association of biosynthetic activity with chloroplasts might be expected, as this is the source of energy in the form of ATP and reducing power in the form of NADPH—both of which are needed for biosynthetic reactions. It would appear that in non-green plastids, these biosynthetic reactions have been retained, even though they require an external source of these cofactors. The presence of this extra compartment for the biosynthetic activity in plant cells imposes different regulatory controls on the metabolism as compared with animal cells, in which most of the biosynthetic activity is located in the cytosol.

A fourth factor that differentiates plant metabolism from that in animals concerns the mitochondrion. Although the basic function of this organelle is the same in both types of organism, plant mitochondria appear to be more involved in biosynthetic activity, in contrast with those of animals, where their almost exclusive function is energy transduction. Hence, in plants there is much more traffic of metabolites through the encompassing envelope of the mitochondrion. The plant mitochondrion can also oxidize NADH from the cytosol and has the alternative oxidase that can allow biosynthetic activity to occur even under very reducing conditions where the tricarboxylic acid cycle and the normal electron transport chain are inhibited. Leaf mitochondria are also an essential component of the photorespiratory cycle, and this may constitute the principal activity of the mitochondrion in leaves.

In the following discussion of carbon flux in both photosynthetic and non-photosynthetic tissues, the uniqueness of plant metabolism must always be kept in mind.

6.2 The hexose phosphate pool

There is always a tendency in textbooks to draw metabolic pathways as simple linear sequences with the starting material at one end and the product at the other. In some cases the pathway may be drawn as a cycle with metabolites flowing in a circle. This may be a convenient way of presenting the material but it is not strictly accurate, especially in plants.

During metabolism there is a flux of metabolites through the various pathways and, in that respect, they can be drawn as linear sequences. However, it must always be remembered that the majority of reactions in the cell are reversible. The enzymes catalysing reversible reactions keep the metabolites upon which they act at equilibrium. Hence, we can imagine the cell as having a series of pools of metabolites, each consisting of a number of compounds that are constantly being interconverted. From these pools various metabolic pathways withdraw metabolites. These are replenished by other pathways that feed compounds into the pools. The hexose phosphates are an example of such a metabolic pool, which is shown in Figure 6.1.

The pool consists of glucose 1-phosphate, glucose 6-phosphate and fructose 6-phosphate. The first two are kept at equilibrium by phosphoglucomutase, and the second two by hexose phosphate isomerase. Metabolites can enter the pool by the breakdown of sucrose or starch and by the gluconeogenic conversion of trioses which in green tissue will mainly come from photosynthesis. Hexose phosphates may leave the pool by conversion into storage products such as starch, by the formation of a transport metabolite (usually sucrose), during the synthesis of cell wall components or by the action of the glycolytic and pentose phosphate

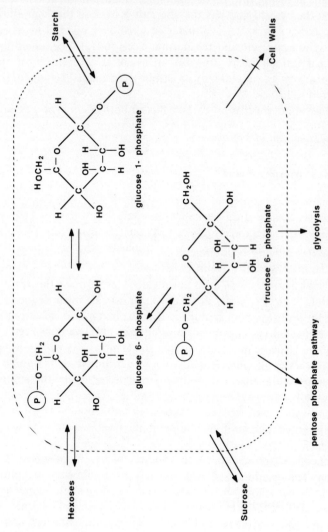

Figure 6.1 The hexose phosphate pool of metabolites. Although this is drawn as a feature in the cell, it must be remembered that the pool is located in the soluble phase of the cell, the cytosol, and is not physically separated from the other metabolites in the cytosol.

pathways. We might anticipate, therefore, that the enzymes catalysing the reactions involved in the entry or exit of metabolites from this pool will be regulated. To make the situation more complex, there are two pools of hexose phosphate in the plant cell; one located in the cytosol and one in the plastids. These two pools are not in direct contact, as the transport systems that move metabolites across the plastid membrane do not recognize hexose phosphates.

6.3 Entry of metabolites into the hexose phosphate pool

6.3.1 The degradation of sucrose

Sucrose is the principal transport carbohydrate in the majority of plants (Akazawa and Okamoto, 1980; Stitt and Steup, 1985). It is also used as a storage material in some plants such as the roots of carrot and the stems of the sugar cane. In these cases, the site of storage is the vacuole of the cell. Sucrose is metabolized by conversion to its component hexoses, glucose and fructose, and this can be accomplished by two routes. The first involves a simple hydrolytic cleavage to the two hexoses by the enzyme invertase:

$$\text{sucrose} + H_2O \rightarrow \text{fructose} + \text{glucose}$$

The standard free energy change of this reaction is -28 kJ/mol and hence the equilibrium lies very much to the right. Invertase is found particularly in young growing tissue where the sucrose is being rapidly metabolized to provide a source of energy and raw materials for cell growth. It is also found in developing oilseeds where the sucrose is used for the synthesis of storage oil.

The second mechanism of sucrose degradation is by the enzyme sucrose synthase which, as the name implies, was originally thought to be used for the biosynthesis of sucrose, but it is now accepted as being used only for its degradation. The reaction catalysed by sucrose synthase is as follows:

$$\text{sucrose} + \text{UDP} \leftrightarrow \text{fructose} + \text{UDP-glucose}$$

There is little free energy change during this reaction and hence it is reversible, unlike the invertase reaction. In other words the energy that would be liberated in the normal hydrolysis of sucrose is conserved in the formation of the phosphate ester bond between UDP and the 1-position of glucose. UDP-glucose can be utilized as such in the formation of cell wall components or it can readily be converted into glucose 1-phosphate, as described below, and hence enter the hexose phosphate pool directly without the utilization of ATP to phosphorylate the free hexoses.

6.3.2 The degradation of starch

The degradation of starch is made complex by the fact that starch is stored in plastids as starch grains. This storage may be of two types. There is a temporary storage in chloroplasts that occurs when the rate of photosynthesis is in excess of the capacity of the cell to utilize the photosynthate. This starch is degraded in the dark. Starch can also be stored on a more permanent basis in storage organs such as tubers and seeds, in another form of plastid called an amyloplast. In both cases, the initial products of starch degradation are released into the plastid and have to be utilized by the plastid or transported across the plastid membrane for use in the cytosol.

Starch is a complex structure, and exists in two forms. The first, amylose, is a straight-chain polymer of α-1,4 linked glucose units. The second form of starch, termed amylopectin, consists of straight chains of α-1,4 linked glucose units, to which side chains are attached. These side chains are also α-1,4 linked glucose polymers which are bonded to the main chain by α-1,6 linkages (Figure 6.2). Hence, amylopectin develops a complex

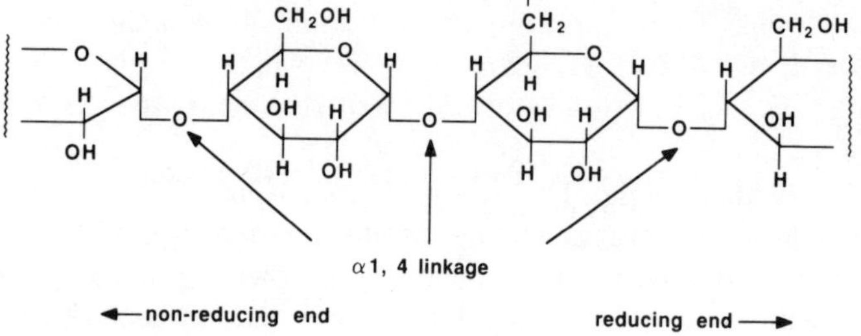

Figure 6.2 The structure of a segment of an amylopectin molecule. The α-1,4 and the α-1,6-glycosidic bonds are indicated.

branched structure. The ratio of amylopectin to amylose can vary considerably in different plants, and this can change the properties of the starch extracted from various plants.

The enzymes that are primarily involved in starch degradation are inhibited in their action by the presence of the α-1,6 bonds and will stop their action when they are about five residues away from this bond. For the whole starch grain to be degraded, the α-1,6 linkages have first to be removed by a debranching enzyme that cleaves this bond and moves the side chain to the end of a straight chain where an α-1,4 linkage is formed. Hence, one long α-1,4 linked chain is formed from a branched chain. This can then be cleaved by the basic enzymes of starch degradation to form the sugars that can enter the hexose phosphate pool. (See Preiss (1982), Preiss and Levi (1980), Stitt and Steup (1985).)

6.3.2.1 α-Amylases. There are two principal enzymatic routes by which starch can be degraded to simple sugars. These are similar in some respects to the routes involved in the degradation of sucrose. The first is the enzyme α-amylase that cleaves the α-1,4 bonds within the amylose chains. This cleavage of the chain continues until the enzyme is inhibited by the α-1,6 linkages, at which point the reaction slows down considerably. The sugars produced by the action of α-amylase are, therefore, maltotriose and maltose (with three and two glucose units respectively) and small amounts of glucose itself. In addition, from amylopectin there remains a highly branched polymer with five or six residues on each side chain. This is termed a limit dextrin. The action of the debranching enzyme converts the limit dextrin into straight chains that can then be further degraded. α-Amylase will not break down the starch to glucose completely; the final steps are accomplished by α-glycosidase.

There is a second amylase, β-amylase, which is especially important in germinating seeds although it is also found in other tissues. This enzyme cleaves off maltose units from the end of the chains until a limit dextrin is formed.

6.3.2.2 Phosphorylase. The second mechanism of starch breakdown occurs through the action of phosphorylase. In this reaction, glucose residues are removed one at a time from the non-reducing end of the amylose molecule. In the reaction, inorganic phosphate is used instead of water to cleave the glycosidic bond with the formation of glucose 1-phosphate. Hence, this reaction conserves the energy of the α-1,4 glycosidic bond. The reaction of phosphorylase is shown below:

$$Phosphate + starch_n \leftrightarrow glucose\ 1\text{-phosphate} + starch_{n-1}$$

The reaction is readily reversible, but the cellular concentration of phosphate is high relative to that of glucose 1-phosphate so that the normal reaction in the cell is in the direction of the degradation of starch.

Phosphorylase appears not to act on intact starch grains. The initial attack is probably via an amylase that releases soluble oligosaccharides which are then acted upon by the phosphorylase. As is the case with α-amylase, the phosphorylase will not cleave near an α-1,6 bond so that the action of the debranching enzyme is essential. Phosphorylase will degrade amylose molecules until the chain length is reduced to four glucose residues when the reaction rate is reduced considerably. An enzyme termed the D-enzyme will take these small fragments and join them together to make larger amylose chains upon which the phosphorylase can continue to act.

6.3.2.3 The control of starch degradation. The analogous storage material in animals to starch is glycogen, which has a structure very similar to that of starch, except that it is more highly branched. The biosynthesis and degradation of glycogen is highly regulated not only by cellular metabolites but also by external signals such as hormones. Glycogen is degraded by the animal phosphorylase that can be phosphorylated or dephosphorylated rendering the enzyme active or inactive respectively. This phosphorylation and dephosphorylation is under the control of hormones via the intermediate, cyclic AMP, which activates a protein kinase.

The plant phosphorylase has a structure almost identical to that of the animal enzyme, except that the area involved in the phosphorylation of the animal enzyme is missing. Nor is there any allosteric regulation of the plant enzyme. Similarly, no regulation of the amylases has been described. It is obvious that regulation of starch degradation in plants must occur, since the enzymes of degradation are present even when starch is not being degraded. It has been suggested that, since phosphorylase requires phosphate as a substrate, the level of phosphate may be the controlling factor. Phosphate concentration increases in the dark and in times of high metabolic activity in cells, and hence would signal the need for starch breakdown. The pH of the plastid stroma may be an additional factor, since the amylases have their highest activity at relatively low pH, another indicator of the need for starch mobilization. However, these controls are crude compared with the sophisticated control of the animal enzyme.

6.3.3 The phosphorylation of free hexoses

The action of invertase, sucrose synthase and the amylases results in the formation of glucose and fructose in the cell (ap Rees, 1980). These must be phosphorylated before they can enter the hexose phosphate pool. This is accomplished by the enzyme hexokinase, which catalyses the following reaction:

$$\text{hexose} + \text{ATP} \leftrightarrow \text{hexose 6-phosphate} + \text{ADP}$$

The reaction has a standard free energy change of $-17\,\text{kJ/mol}$ and hence favours the direction of hexose phosphate synthesis. The situation with regard to hexokinase in plants is complex; there are at least three hexokinases in plant cells, probably with different functions. There is a cytosolic enzyme that will phosphorylate both glucose and fructose as well as other hexoses. There is also a hexokinase bound to the outer membrane of the mitochondrion, which preferentially phosphorylates glucose. The exact function of this hexokinase is not known. A similar if not identical enzyme is found in animals where it has been postulated to react with the newly formed ATP as it is leaving the mitochondrion and hence takes precedence in the use of the ATP. This may function in the control of oxidative phosphorylation in the mitochondrion by generating ADP which can immediately re-enter the mitochondrion and be re-phosphorylated. The amount of this hexokinase bound to the membrane of the mitochondrion is controlled by the concentration of glucose 6-phosphate in the cell. Hence, at high concentrations of glucose 6-phosphate little of this hexokinase is bound to the membrane and the enzyme has then to compete with the other reactions in the cell for ATP.

Some plants have a third hexokinase in their plastids, but this may not be universally the case and may depend to a large extent on the tissue in which the plastid is found. In chloroplasts the concentration of free hexoses should be small, so the need for a hexokinase may be limited. The principal transport of sugars across the plastid membrane is by the phosphate translocator which transports triose phosphates. From these, hexose phosphates can be formed directly. In plastids involved in other functions, for example fatty acid biosynthesis in oilseeds, there may be some transport of hexose across the plastid membrane which would require an enzyme within the plastid. In all tissues studied there appears to be a number of distinct hexokinases whose function and cellular location has not so far been determined.

6.4. Exit of metabolites from the hexose phosphate pool

6.4.1 The synthesis of sucrose

It was originally though that sucrose was the immediate end product of photosynthesis and hence was produced in the chloroplast. It is now accepted that the end product of photosynthesis is actually triose phosphate, which is transported across the chloroplast membrane into the cytosol by the phosphate translocator. If the supply of triose phosphate exceeds the metabolic needs of the cell, the triose phosphate is converted to hexose phosphate by the enzymes aldolase and fructose 1,6-bisphosphatase and hence enters the hexose phosphate pool in the cytosol. The concentration of this pool in the cytosol appears to be a major factor in the control of the synthesis of sucrose.

There are two enzymes that could be involved in sucrose synthesis; sucrose synthase, described above, and sucrose phosphate synthase. It is now thought that only the latter is used by the cell for synthesis. This enzyme catalyses the following reaction:

$$\text{UDP-glucose} + \text{fructose 6-phosphate} \leftrightarrow \text{UDP} + \text{sucrose-phosphate}$$

A second enzyme, sucrose phosphate phosphatase, cleaves the phosphate from the sucrose phosphate to release the free sucrose. Overall, UDP-glucose and fructose 6-phosphate are condensed to form UDP, phosphate and sucrose. The overall equilibrium position for these two reactions greatly favours sucrose synthesis, in contrast to sucrose synthase which is readily reversible. Ultimately, the loss of free energy during this reaction results from the fact that fructose 6-phosphate is used in the reaction instead of fructose. It is the hydrolysis of this bond in the sucrose phosphate that drives the reaction to the right. It is for this reason, and the fact that the concentration of sucrose phosphate synthase correlates well with the level of sucrose synthesis, that this enzyme is thought to be the one involved in sucrose synthesis.

Sucrose phosphate synthase is a regulatory enzyme, although it does not show the degree of regulation that might be expected of an enzyme so central to plant metabolism. The enzyme is activated by glucose 6-phosphate. The concentration of this metabolite is an indication of the status of the hexose phosphate pool, so it might be expected that, as the level of the pool increases, sucrose synthesis would be favoured. The enzyme is also inhibited by inorganic phosphate which would indicate the need for hexose phosphates to be used for energy metabolism instead of sucrose synthesis. The UDP-glucose/phosphate and the fructose 6-phosphate/phosphate ratios appear to be particularly important in its regulation. Sucrose synthesis has been reviewed by Akazawa and Okomoto (1980); Stitt and Steup (1985).

6.4.2 The synthesis of starch

Until the early 1960s it was assumed that starch biosynthesis occurred by the reverse reaction of phosphorylase but, as discussed above, the concentrations of substrates and products for this reaction in the cell make it unlikely that this enzyme contributes at all to starch synthesis (see reviews by Preiss, 1982; Preiss and Levi, 1980).

In the early 1960s the importance of the sugar derivatives of UDP in the biosynthesis of polysaccharides became clear. In animals, it was shown that glycogen was synthesized from UDP-glucose and it was assumed that, since starch was very similar to glycogen, starch would also be formed from this precursor. The enzyme that adds glucose to the amylose chains is starch synthase, and this enzyme will use UDP-glucose. However, another precursor, ADP-glucose, is a much more effective substrate and is now accepted as the precursor. Why should the synthesis of starch differ in this way from that of glycogen?

Starch is only one of a number of polymers of glucose that are formed in plant cells in large amounts. Plant cell walls are composed of polyglucans as well as other polyhexans and polypentans. All these polymers are derived from UDP-glucose. During cell growth a major flux of carbon may be passing through UDP-glucose for cell wall biosynthesis. Hence, it makes sense for the biosynthesis of starch, which is so important for the energy metabolism of the cell, to be separated from cell wall biosynthesis, and regulated independently. In animals, where the cells are not surrounded by a cell wall, this separation is not necessary.

Starch synthase is not regulated but the synthesis of its substrate ADP-glucose is under tight control. ADP-glucose is synthesized by ADP-glucose pyrophosphorylase which catalyses the following reaction:

$$\text{ATP} + \text{glucose 1-phosphate} \leftrightarrow \text{ADP-glucose} + \text{PPi}$$

Hence, the synthesis of starch draws directly on the hexose phosphate pool. The enzyme is powerfully activated by phosphoglycerate, the first product of photosynthetic carbon fixation. The presence of high concentrations of phosphoglycerate indicates active photosynthesis, which, in turn, would make starch synthesis possible. In contrast, inorganic phosphate inhibits the activity of the enzyme. High concentrations of phosphate indicate the need for carbon to be catabolized for the production of ADP, and hence the flow of carbon into starch should be stopped. The synthesis of starch is therefore regulated in a manner that is consistent with starch being synthesized when the supply of carbon is abundant, and inhibited when carbon is being utilized for other purposes.

6.4.3 Cell wall biosynthesis

A further drain on the hexose phosphate pool, especially during cell growth, is the biosynthesis of cell walls (Ericson and Elbein, 1980; Feingold and Avigad, 1980). The basic starting component for cell wall biosynthesis for all polysaccharides appears to be UDP-glucose. This is converted into other hexose and pentose derivatives of UDP for polymerization into the various hexans and pentans that make up the polysaccharides of the wall. UDP-glucose is also the precursor of UDP-galacturonic acid for pectin biosynthesis. The mechanism by which cell wall biosynthesis is controlled is as yet unknown.

6.5 The glycolytic and pentose phosphate pathways

6.5.1 Introduction

The glycolytic and pentose phosphate pathways are normally considered to be independent. However, they are interlinked and both can supply trioses for further metabolism. At times the pathways may act in the classical way depicted in textbooks, but at other times they may not be so independent. Hence, they will be considered together as a means of linking the hexose and pentose phosphate pools under the different conditions found in the cell.

6.5.2 The conversion of fructose 6-phosphate to triose phosphate

The conversion of fructose 6-phosphate to triose phosphate, shown in Figure 6.3, is the initial part of the classical glycolytic pathway (ap Rees, 1980; 1985). The first reaction of this pathway is catalysed by the enzyme phosphofructokinase:

fructose 6-phosphate + ATP↔fructose 1,6-bisphosphate + ADP

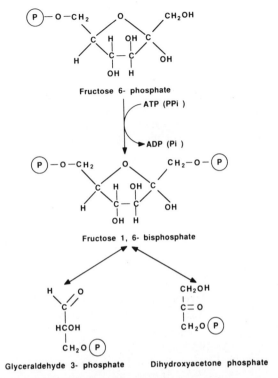

Fructose 6- phosphate

Fructose 1, 6- bisphosphate

Glyceraldehyde 3- phosphate   Dihydroxyacetone phosphate

Figure 6.3 The conversion of fructose 6-phosphate to the trioses, glyceraldehyde 3-phosphate and dihydroxyacetone phosphate. The first reaction can be catalysed by two enzymes in plants; an ATP-dependent phosphofructokinase that utilizes ATP as the phosphoryl donor with the formation of ADP, and a pyrophosphate (PPi) dependent phosphofructokinase that utilizes PPi as the phosphoryl donor with the formation of inorganic phosphate.

The standard free energy change of this reaction is $-14\,kJ/mol$ and hence the reaction can be considered as being practically irreversible under physiological conditions. The enzyme is under tight regulatory control in all organisms because it catalyses a reaction that drains metabolites from the hexose phosphate pool. Unfortunately, our knowledge of this enzyme in plants is limited. However, the plant enzyme does show regulatory control. The enzyme is powerfully inhibited by phosphoenolpyruvate (PEP) and to a lesser extent by ATP. It is clear, therefore, that this enzyme is principally controlled by the energy needs of the cell. In animals, phosphofructokinase is inhibited by ATP and activated by AMP so that the ATP/AMP ratio is very important. In plants, neither AMP nor ADP has any effect on the enzyme at normal cellular concentrations. However, inorganic phosphate is a very powerful activator, so the ATP/Pi ratio is more important. The inhibition by PEP is also relieved by inorganic phosphate, and since PEP is such a powerful inhibitor it is probably the PEP/Pi ratio that is of prime importance in the regulation of this step in glycolysis.

Until recently, it was considered that the reaction catalysed by phosphofructokinase was the only means by which hexose phosphates could enter the initial part of the glycolytic pathway. However, a different enzyme has now been discovered that uses pyrophosphate as the phosphoryl donor to fructose 6-phosphate. This enzyme is found only in plants and a few bacteria, and has never been described in animals. It catalyses the following reaction:

$$\text{fructose 6-phosphate} + \text{PPi} \leftrightarrow \text{fructose 1,6-bisphosphate} + \text{Pi}$$

Unlike the ATP-dependent enzyme, the pyrophosphate-dependent phosphofructokinase is reversible under physiological conditions. It could, therefore, function in the reversal of glycolysis for the formation of starch or sucrose. However, the concentration of fructose 1,6-bisphosphatase is usually high enough that a second enzyme would seem to be redundant.

If one considers the enzyme as a component of the glycolytic pathway one is faced with a second dilemma. In most cases, it is considered that the concentration of pyrophosphate is kept very low in the cell, and it has been postulated that this is essential if biosynthetic reactions such as that catalysed by the UDPG and ADPG pyrophosphorylases are to have equilibria that favour the formation of products. It has been accepted for a long time that a pyrophosphatase is present in cells to hydrolyse any pyrophosphate that is formed. However, the concentration of pyrophosphate has been measured, and found to be high enough that the pyrophosphate phosphofructokinase could be active, allowing the enzyme to have a function in glycolysis.

The pyrophosphate enzyme is found in highest concentration in young active tissues in which pyrophosphate may be generated in large amounts by biosynthetic reactions. The enzyme could, therefore, be a means of conserving the energy that is released on hydrolysis of the acid anhydride bond in pyrophosphate.

A final property of this enzyme is that it is activated by fructose 2,6-bisphosphate at very low concentrations. This compound was discovered in rat liver as an activator of the ATP-dependent phosphofructokinase. In contrast, the ATP-dependent enzyme in plants is not affected. The synthesis of fructose 2,6-bisphosphate is highly regulated, and in plants is an indicator of a tissue that has high metabolic activity.

At the moment, the function of the pyrophosphate enzyme is not known. Since it is present in high concentrations and is regulated by fructose 2,6-bisphosphate, one can assume that it has a very important function in plant metabolism that has still to be elucidated.

The product of the phosphofructokinase reaction, fructose 1,6-bis-phosphate, is cleaved by the enzyme aldolase giving rise to the two trioses, dihydroxyacetone phosphate and glyceraldehyde 3-phosphate. This enzyme in plants appears to be very similar to the enzyme from other sources. The standard free energy change in this reaction is $+22\,kJ/mol$, and hence the reaction favours fructose 1,6-bisphosphate. Under cellular conditions, however, it has been suggested that the equilibrium is more in favour of the trioses than might be concluded from the standard free energy change, so that the reaction is reversible. This results from the fact that there is a single substrate and two products, which is important at low concentrations as compared with standard concentrations.

The two trioses are kept in equilibrium by the enzyme triose phosphate isomerase which is always present in large amounts in cells. The standard free energy change in this reaction is $+7.5\,kJ/mol$, and hence the equilibrium is in favour of dihydroxyacetone phosphate. The fact that aldolase and triose phosphate isomerase both have equilibria that are not in favour of glyceraldehyde 3-phosphate should be kept in mind, since this metabolite is used both in the glycolytic pathway and in the pentose phosphate pathways.

6.5.3 The formation of pentoses by the oxidative reactions of the pentose phosphate pathway

The pentose phosphate pathway is normally presented as a cyclic pathway in which glucose 6-phosphate is converted by a series of reactions back to fructose 6-phosphate (see ap Rees, 1985). In the process carbon dioxide is liberated and NADPH formed. Undoubtedly the pathway can operate in this manner, but it is more useful to consider it in two parts. The first part is the series of reactions in which glucose 6-phosphate is oxidized to ribulose 5-phosphate with the formation of NADPH from $NADP^+$. The second is a series of reversible reactions that serve to equilibrate hexoses, pentoses, a heptulose, a tetrose and the trioses.

The reactions of the oxidative pentose phosphate pathway are shown in Figure 6.4. The first reaction is catalysed by glucose 6-phosphate

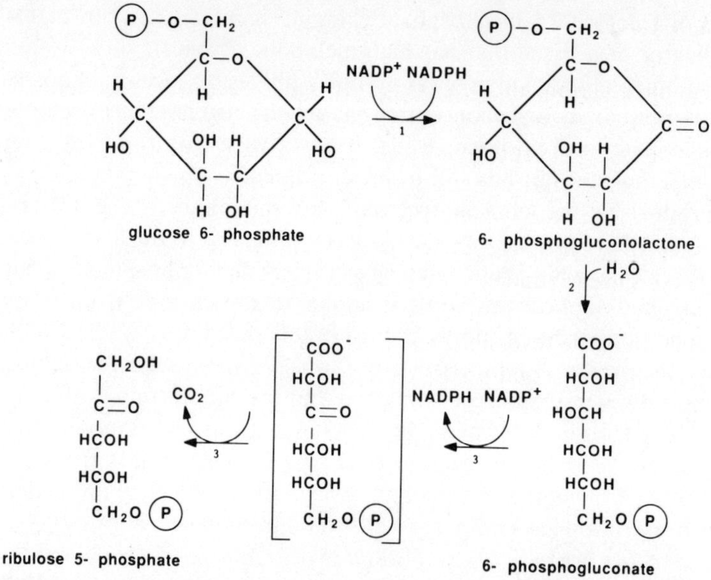

Figure 6.4 The formation of ribulose 5-phosphate from glucose 6-phosphate by the oxidative reactions of the pentose phosphate pathway. The enzymes catalysing these reactions are; (1) glucose 6-phosphate dehydrogenase, (2) 6-phosphogluconolactonase, (3) 6-phosphogluconate dehydrogenase.

dehydrogenase and forms phosphogluconolactone from glucose 6-phosphate with the generation of NADPH from $NADP^+$. The lactone is very unstable, and a lactonase converts it to phosphogluconate. Phosphogluconate is further oxidized by phosphogluconate dehydrogenase to ribulose 5-phosphate, a reaction that liberates carbon dioxide and also converts a further molecule of $NADP^+$ into NADPH. Overall these reactions are irreversible.

The function of this pathway is to generate NADPH that is required for biosynthetic reactions. Hence, this segment of the pathway will be most active in plant tissues that are very actively growing. A number of metabolites have been proposed as regulators of these reactions, but undoubtedly the most important is the cell's requirement for NADPH. NADPH is a product of two of the reactions and will inhibit each reaction as its concentration increases. The ratio of the substrate to the product, that is the $NADP^+/NADPH$ ratio, will determine the velocity of the two reactions and will regulate the flux through this segment of the pathway.

6.5.4 *The reversible reactions of the pentose phosphate pathway*

The reversible reactions of the pentose phosphate pathway are shown in Figure 6.5. This pathway serves to interconvert the pentoses—ribulose 5-phosphate, ribose 5-phosphate, xylulose 5-phosphate; a hexose—fructose 6-phosphate; a heptulose—sedoheptulose 7-phosphate; a tetrose—erythrose 4-phosphate and two trioses—glyceraldehyde 3-phosphate and dihydroxyacetone phosphate. The enzymes catalysing these reactions are indicated in Figure 6.5 and will not be discussed further (see ap Rees (1980; 1985)).

The function of the reversible reactions of the pathway is to keep all the above metabolites at equilibrium. Under conditions in which there is a high demand for NADPH, the pathway will act as a cycle to convert

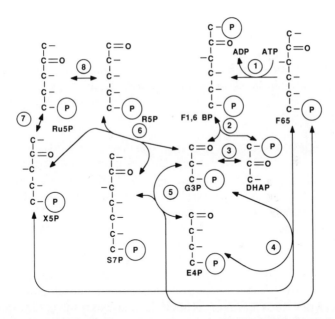

Figure 6.5 The reversible reactions of the pentose phosphate pathway. To simplify the diagram, the hydrogen atoms of the molecules have been omitted and the —OH groups are indicated by a single line. The aldehyde or keto groups are represented by a double-bonded oxygen. The abbreviations used are: Ru5P, ribulose 5-phosphate; X5P, xylulose 5-phosphate; R5P, ribose 5-phosphate; S7P, sedoheptulose 7-phosphate; G3P, glyceraldehyde 3-phosphate; E4P, erythrose 4-phosphate; DHAP, dihydroxyacetone phosphate; F6P, fructose 6-phosphate. The enzymes catalysing the reactions are: (1) phosphofructokinase, (2) fructose 1,6-bisphosphate aldolase, (3) triosephosphate isomerase, (4) transketolase, (5) transaldolase, (6) transketolase, (7) ribulose 5-phosphate 3-epimerase, (8) ribose 5-phosphate isomerase.

ribulose 5-phosphate, the product of the oxidative reactions, to fructose 6-phosphate. However, the metabolites of the pathway are also used as starting points for other pathways. Ribose 5-phosphate is required for nucleic acid biosynthesis, and the supply of this metabolite may at times be a major function of these reactions. Erythrose 4-phosphate is a starting metabolite of the shikimate pathway which results in the synthesis of aromatic amino acids. Not only are these amino acids essential for protein biosynthesis, they are also used in the formation of the cell wall component, lignin, and for other phenolics that may have a role in defence against pathogens. Under some conditions, therefore, the pathway may function to produce this component. If the flux through the oxidative reactions is insufficient to meet the cell's needs for ribose 5-phosphate and erythrose 4-phosphate, it is probable that the reactions will run in the reverse direction to that normally depicted in textbooks and will start with fructose 6-phosphate.

It must also be remembered that one of the metabolites of the pathway is glyceraldehyde 3-phosphate, which is the starting component for the oxidative reactions of the glycolytic pathway. The flux through the pathway from ribulose 5-phosphate will often be into the glycolytic pathway, since it is likely that under conditions where NADPH is being utilized ATP will also be required.

6.6 The oxidative and ATP-generating reactions of glycolysis

The reactions for the conversion of glyceraldehyde 3-phosphate to pyruvate are shown in Figure 6.6. The reactions of this part of the pathway are a remarkable example of evolutionary engineering, in that the structures of the compounds involved are manipulated to generate compounds of a high free energy of hydrolysis that can be used for the synthesis of ATP.

The first two reactions of the pathway, catalysed by the glyceraldehyde 3-phosphate dehydrogenase and 3-phosphoglycerate kinase, have been studied extensively as an example of substrate-level phosphorylation, and have been described previously. These two reactions result in the synthesis of one molecule of glyceraldehyde 3-phosphate oxidized. The reaction also generates one molecule of ATP per molecule of NADH. Under aerobic conditions this NADH can be oxidized by the mitochondrial external dehydrogenase, as described earlier, to yield a further two molecules of ATP.

Under anaerobic conditions this NADH has to be oxidized back to NAD^+ or the substrate-level generation of ATP will be inhibited. Under

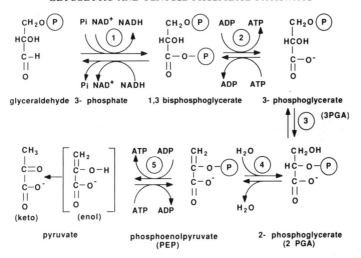

Figure 6.6 The oxidative reactions of the glycolytic pathway. The enzymes catalysing these reactions are; (1) glyceraldehyde 3-phosphate dehydrogenase, (2) 3-phosphoglycerate kinase, (3) phosphoglyceromutase, (4) enolase, (5) pyruvate kinase.

these conditions substrate-level ATP synthesis is essential for the cell, which means that the regeneration of NAD^+ is of critical importance. The overall standard free energy change of these two reactions is $-13\,kJ/mol$, and hence the equilibrium position favours 3-phosphogly-cerate. The equilibrium position of these reactions, therefore, tends to overcome the unfavourable equilibria of the aldolase and triose phosphate isomerase reactions.

Glyceraldehyde 3-phosphate dehydrogenase is at a branchpoint of metabolism as it drains metabolites from various pools that are in equilibrium into a pathway that in the cytosol is committed to triose oxidation. This enzyme is not regulated except by the ratio of $NAD^+/NADH$. However, as will be seen later, in the tricarboxylic acid cycle this ratio is of great importance in the control of plant metabolism.

The next two reactions, those that convert 3-phosphoglycerate to phosphoenolpyruvate, are catalysed by phosphoglyceromutase and enolase and are readily reversible. These reactions serve to convert a phosphate ester bond from one that has a low free energy of hydrolysis to a high-energy one. The phosphate ester bond in 3-phosphoglycerate has a standard free energy change that is typical of phosphate esters $(-14\,kJ/mol)$. By moving the phosphate group to the 2 position of the molecule, then dehydrating it to form PEP, the phosphate ester bond is placed next to a double bond. The standard free energy of hydrolysis of the phosphate group now becomes $-54\,\text{kJ/mol}$. In the following reaction, catalysed by pyruvate kinase, the phosphate group is transferred to ADP with the formation of ATP in a reaction that has a standard free energy change of $-31\,\text{kJ/mol}$. The actual product of the reaction is pyruvate in the enol form, but this is very unstable and rearranges to the keto form which cannot accept a phosphate group. Hence, the reaction of pyruvate kinase is virtually irreversible.

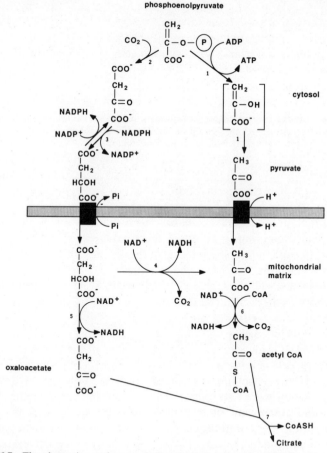

Figure 6.7 The alternative pathways of phosphoenolpyruvate metabolism. The enzymes involved are; (1) pyruvate kinase, (2) phosphoenolpyruvate carboxylase; (3) malate dehydrogenase, (4) NAD-specific malic enzyme, (5) malate dehydrogenase, (6) pyruvate dehydrogenase complex, (7) citrate synthase.

PEP is at a branch point in metabolism which is even more important in plants than in animals. As has been mentioned before, a large percentage of the flux through the above pathways may be to supply carbon compounds for biosynthetic activity, which is much more predominant in plants than it is in animals. This will be evident in the following section in the discussion of the tricarboxylic acid cycle.

6.7 The utilization of phosphoenolpyruvate (PEP) in plants

From PEP there are two routes into the tricarboxylic acid cycle (Figure 6.7 (Davies,1979)). The route most commonly illustrated is that through pyruvate kinase described above. In animals, pyruvate kinase is a highly regulated enzyme but such regulation has not been described in plants. However, measurements of the concentrations of PEP and pyruvate in plant cells indicate that the enzyme is not at equilibrium so that the reaction must be controlled. The enzyme is inhibited by one of the products, ATP, and the ATP/ADP ratio may be important in its regulation.

A second route for PEP metabolism is via the enzyme phosphoenol-pyruvate carboxylase. This enzyme forms oxaloacetate from PEP and bicarbonate. In turn the oxaloacetate is converted to malate by malate dehydrogenase, a reaction that requires NADP and liberates $NADP^+$. Phosphoenolpyruvate carboxylase bypasses the ATP-generating step of pyruvate kinase and allows carbon to enter the mitochondrial reactions even at high ATP levels.

6.8 The utilization of pyruvate

6.8.1 Introduction

Pyruvate is also at a branch point in metabolism, and can be used in a number of ways depending upon the requirements of the cell. The most direct use for pyruvate is its transamination to form the amino acid alanine, an essential component of proteins. Plants are obligate aerobes, and need oxygen for their continued growth. However, they can survive periods of anaerobic conditions and under these conditions the pyruvate is metabolized to ethanol to regenerate the NAD^+ required by glycolysis. Under aerobic conditions, the pyruvate can enter the mitochondrion where it can be oxidized by the tricarboxylic acid cycle.

6.8.2 Anaerobic utilization of pyruvate

The majority of plants have a limited tolerance to anaerobic conditions, although in general they can survive to some extent. In some cases, however, plants can show a remarkable tolerance. For example, young rice seedlings can survive totally submerged and even show a limited amount of growth. Plants growing in marshes have to tolerate anaerobic conditions in their roots and may also have to survive periodic flooding. It is clear that the ability to survive these conditions is very variable, and some plants are especially well adapted.

Under anaerobic conditions the accumulation of NADH and lack of NAD^+ inhibits glycolysis and hence a pathway must exist for the regeneration of NAD^+. In animals, this is accomplished by the enzyme lactate dehyrogenase that converts pyruvate into lactate:

$$\text{pyruvate} + \text{NADH} \leftrightarrow \text{lactate} + NAD^+$$

The NAD^+ is regenerated and the lactate removed by the bloodstream. Hence, glycolysis can continue to function and generate ATP for the cell metabolism. Some plants possess lactate dehydrogenase, and it is assumed that this mechanism of NAD^+ regeneration can be used at times. The disposal of the lactate, however, poses a special problem for plants.

Although other mechanisms of anaerobic metabolism have been proposed, it is likely that the main one is the conversion of pyruvate to ethanol. Pyruvate is converted to ethanol by two reactions, pyruvate decarboxylase and alcohol dehydrogenase:

$$\text{pyruvate} \leftrightarrow \text{acetaldehyde} + CO_2$$
$$\text{acetaldehyde} + \text{NADH} \leftrightarrow \text{ethanol} + NAD^+$$

Ethanol is toxic to plants, but it diffuses rapidly and its movement is not impeded by the membranes of the cell. Hence, even under prolonged anaerobiosis, glycolysis operates and the final product of the pathway, ethanol, can be excreted by the tissue into the surrounding medium—a process that is somewhat analogous to the excretion of lactate in animals.

The action of pyruvate decarboxylase must be controlled so that pyruvate is decarboxylated only under anaerobic conditions. The importance of pH in the control of plant enzymes has been emphasized by Davies (1979) and appears to play a role here. Pyruvate decarboxylase has a acid pH optimum for activity, and under normal cellular conditions (pH 7.0) it is virtually inactive. It is possible that the first reponse to anaerobic conditions is the activity of lactate dehydrogenase. This produces lactate, which in turn lowers the pH of the cytosol. Under these conditions the pyruvate decarboxylase would be activated and ethanol production would commence.

6.8.3 Pyruvate utilization by the mitochondrion

6.8.3.1 Pyruvate transport into the mitochondrion. The outer membrane of the mitochondrion contains pores large enough to allow molecules with molecular weights of up to 10 000 to pass through. This membrane, therefore, does not pose any resistance to the passage of pyruvate. The inner membrane is quite different, and is highly selective in the molecules that can pass through it. Molecules that enter the mitochondrion are carried on specific carrier proteins, and pyruvate is no exception to this. This uptake of pyruvate is driven by the proton gradient that is generated by the electron-transport chain. The uptake of pyruvate is accompanied by the simultaneous transport of a proton and hence is involved in the discharge of the proton gradient. It has been suggested that, under some circumstances, the capacity of the transporter may be limiting for the respiratory needs of the cell.

A second pathway for the accumulation of pyruvate in the mitochondrion is from PEP, as described previously. This pathway leads to the formation of malate that can be rapidly transported into mitochondria. Once inside the mitochondria, this malate can be converted into pyruvate by the malic enzyme. This enzyme converts malate into pyruvate, releasing carbon dioxide and in the process reducing NAD^+ to NADH. In some cases, this could be a major source of pyruvate for the tricarboxylic acid cycle.

6.8.3.2 The oxidation of pyruvate: the pyruvate dehydrogenase complex. As the name implies, the oxidation of pyruvate is catalysed by a series of proteins that form a complex. There are three distinct reactions catalysed by the complex, resulting in the oxidation of pyruvate to acetyl coenzyme A with the release of carbon dioxide and the reduction of NAD^+ to NADH that can be oxidized by the electron-transport chain. The reactions of this complex are shown in Figure 6.8. The energy released by this oxidation is conserved by the formation of NADH and the thioester bond in acetyl CoA. The formation of this latter compound is of extreme importance. The first reaction of the tricarboxylic acid cycle is the condensation of acetyl CoA with oxaloacetic acid to form citrate. The equilibrium position of this

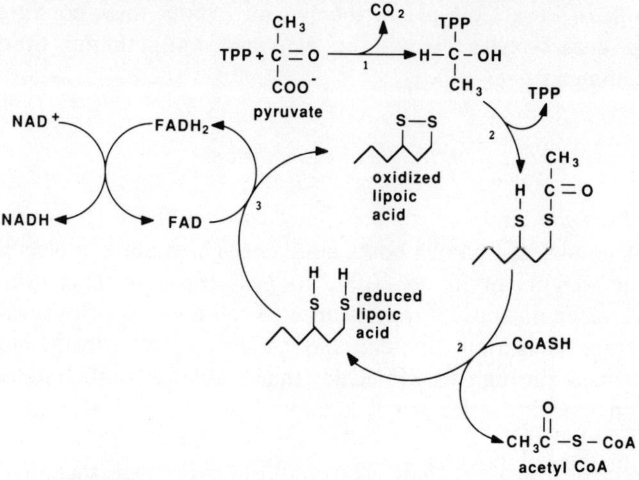

Figure 6.8 The reactions of the pyruvate dehydrogenase complex. Only the terminal portion of the arm that attaches the lipoic acid to the transacylase subunit of the complex is shown. TPP is thiamine pyrophosphate. The enzymes catalysing these reactions are: (1) pyruvate dehydrogenase, (2) transacetylase, (3) lipoic acid dehydrogenase.

reaction favours citrate because of the hydrolysis of the thioester bond of acetyl CoA. Hence the reaction of the pyruvate dehydrogenase complex anticipates the requirement of the following reaction.

The pyruvate dehydrogenase complex catalyses three distinct reactions. The first is catalysed by pyruvate dehydrogenase itself, which catalyses the decarboxylation of pyruvate with the release of carbon dioxide. The acetaldehyde remaining after this decarboxylation is bound to the enzyme through the cofactor thiamine pyrophosphate. At this stage, therefore, there has been no oxidation of the molecule. Pyruvate dehydrogenase consists of two different polypeptides and has the structure $\alpha_2\beta_2$.

The second enzyme of the complex is a transacetylase, which performs several functions. First of all it forms the core of the complex and binds the first enzyme, pyruvate dehydrogenase, and the third enzyme, dihydrolipoamide dehydrogenase. The presence of this enzyme is therefore essential for the stability of the complex. The cofactor attached to the transacetylase is lipoic acid, which is attached to the enzyme through an amide bond to an ε-amino group in a lysine of the polypeptide. This forms a long arm that allows the transacetylase to interact both with the first and with the third enzymes of the complex.

The transacetylase interacts with the pyruvate dehydrogenase to catalyse a complex reaction. The acetaldehyde is oxidized to the level of acetic acid, and in the process the lipoic acid is reduced to dihydrolipoic acid. The acetic acid is not released but is bound to the lipoic acid through a thioester bond. Hence, some of the energy liberated on the oxidation of pyruvate is retained by the formation of this bond. Finally, the transacetylase catalyses a transfer of the acetyl group from the lipoic acid to CoA with the formation of acetyl CoA, the lipoic acid being left in a reduced state. The final reaction of the complex is catalysed by dihydrolipoamide dehydrogenase that reoxidizes the lipoic acid. In the process NAD^+ is reduced to NADH which can be utilized by the electron-transport chain.

Since this complex occupies such an important branch point in metabolism, it must be highly regulated. The principal means, on a short-term basis, appears to be by the $NAD^+/NADH$ ratio. Hence, if ATP is not required by the cell, NADH will not be oxidized by the electron transport chain and will accumulate in the mitochondrial matrix, and the $NAD^+/NADH$ ratio will be lowered. NADH is a powerful inhibitor of dihydrolipoamide dehydrogenase and hence the dihydrolipoic acid will not be reoxidized. In turn, it will be unable to accept further acetyl groups from the pyruvate dehydrogenase and the whole complex will be inhibited.

A second control of the enzyme may be thought of as a longer-term control, although it can sometimes occur very rapidly. The complex contains two other enzymes that are not directly involved in the catalytic reactions of the complex. A kinase is present that will phosphorylate the α subunit of the pyruvate dehydrogenase, rendering the enzyme inactive. This kinase is activated by NADH and acetyl CoA and hence the complex is rendered inactive under conditions when there is no requirement for these metabolites. Obviously, this inactivation of the complex complements the direct inhibition of the NADH. Also attached to the complex is a phosphatase that removes the phosphate from the pyruvate dehydrogenase. The main requirement of this phosphatase is a high concentrations of Mg^{2+}. Most of the magnesium in the cell is complexed to various metabolites such as ATP and the intermediates of the tricarboxylic acid cycle. Hence, if ATP and the intermediates are low, the concentration of free magnesium will be increased, this in turn activates the phosphatase, removing the phosphate from the pyruvate dehydrogenase and allowing metabolites to flow into the tricarboxylic acid cycle.

CHAPTER SEVEN

THE TRICARBOXYLIC ACID CYCLE

7.1 Introduction

The reactions of the tricarboxylic acid cycle in plants are very similar to those found in animals. However, because of the biosynthetic activity of the plant cell the function of the cycle is more complex than in animals, where the cycle functions principally to generate NADH to be used by the electron transport chain for ATP synthesis. In plants, the cycle also generates intermediates for amino acid biosynthesis and for nitrogen assimilation, and is involved in photorespiration in photosynthetic tissue. All these must be kept in mind when discussing the reactions of the cycle.

7.2 The reactions of the tricarboxylic acid cycle

The reactions of the cycle are the same as those described in much more detail in animals and are shown in Figure 7.1 (see Wiskich and Dry (1985), Douce (1985)). All the reactions of the cycle are reversible except for isocitrate dehydrogenase and α-ketoglutarate dehydrogenase. Hence, although the reactions are normally drawn as a cycle there are times when some of the reactions may act in reverse. Also, the main product of the cycle may be intermediates such as α-ketoglutarate, and only part of the cycle may be used in these reactions.

The first reaction of the cycle is the formation of citrate catalysed by citrate synthase. The affinity of this enzyme for its substrates is very high, and hence it is active at very low substrate concentrations. This is essential because the concentration of acetyle CoA and oxaloacetate are low in the mitochondrion. This is particularly true for oxaloacetate because the equilibrium position of the reaction that forms it, catalysed by malate dehydrogenase, favours malate by a large amount; hence, the concentration of oxaloacetate is low.

Since this is the first reaction of the pathway, the enzyme shows

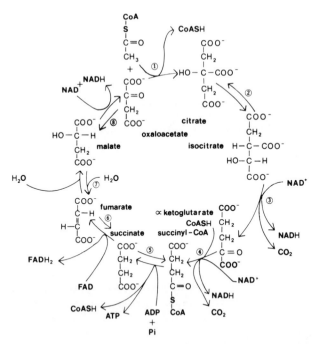

Figure 7.1 The reactions of the tricarboxylic acid cycle. The enzymes catalysing these reaction are; (1) citrate synthase, (2) aconitase, (3) isocitrate dehydrogenase, (4) α-ketoglutarate dehydrogenase, (5) succinate thiokinase, (6) succinate dehydrogenase, (7) fumarase, (8) malate dehydrogenase.

regulatory properties. The enzyme is inhibited by ATP which competes with acetyl CoA at the active site. High concentrations of ATP would indicate that the cycle is not required for energy metabolism. In animals the enzyme is also inhibited by covalent modification. One might expect the animal enzyme to have more complex regulation than the plant enzyme because citrate is exported from animal mitochondria and cleaved by citrate lyase to generate acetyl CoA in the cytosol for fatty acid biosynthesis. Although citrate lyase has been found in some plant tissues, acetyl CoA is normally generated within plastids, where fatty acid biosythesis occurs, and from substrates other than citrate.

Citrate and isocitrate are kept in equilibrium by the enzyme aconitase. This has not been studied to any extent in plants. It is a complex enzyme that in animals contains an iron–sulphur centre which appears to be involved in the regulation of the enzyme, since it does not catalyse an oxidation–reduction reaction. The enzyme acts on the free acids. Citrate is a powerful chelator of metal ions, and its affinity towards magnesium ions is ten times greater than that of isocitrate. Since aconitase will not act on the metal chelates, the concentration of magnesium ion in the mitochondrion will determine the ratio of citrate to isocitrate and may be important in regulating the activity of the cycle.

Isocitrate dehydrogenase catalyses a reaction that is irreversible. It is the main site of regulation of the tricarboxylic acid cycle in animals, where it is regulated by ATP inhibition and ADP activation. This regulation does not occur in plants. The enzyme catalyses the first oxidative step in the cycle, and in the process NAD^+ is converted to NADH. NADH binds more tightly to the enzyme than NAD^+ and inhibits the reaction so that the rate is slowed to 50% of its maximal rate when only 10% of the NAD is in the reduced form. This appears to be the major control of the enzyme in plants. The plant enzyme is also activated by free citrate and isocitrate so the concentration of magnesium in the mitochondrion may also be important, as was suggested earlier.

The first oxidative reaction of the cycle is followed immediately by the second, that is, the oxidation of α-ketoglutarate to succinyl CoA. This reaction is catalysed by a complex very similar to that involved in the oxidation of pyruvate. The α-ketoglutarate dehydrogenase complex has not been studied extensively in plants. The products of the reaction are succinyl CoA and NADH as well as carbon dioxide. Hence, the energy released by the oxidation of α-ketoglutarate is conserved not only by the formation of NADH that can be used by the electron transport chain but also by the formation of the thioester bond in succinyl CoA. The plant enzyme is activated by AMP which may have a role in the regulation of the complex since this would indicate a requirement for ATP. It has also been suggested that the supply of CoA may be limiting in mitochondria and could be involved in controlling the rate of the complex. CoA will be released in the mitochondrion from the utilization of acetyl CoA and the breakdown of succinyl CoA. This latter reaction is reversible and hence under conditions where ATP is not being utilized, CoA could be made unavailable by not being released from succinyl CoA.

The reaction catalysed by succinyl CoA synthetase is freely reversible and, in the cycle, is normally shown to progress in the reverse direction. The hydrolysis of the thioester is coupled to the synthesis of ATP; this is the only place in the tricarboxylic acid cycle where substrate-level phosphorylation occurs and ATP is synthesized directly without the electron transport chain being involved. The enzyme is probably regulated by the supply of substrates.

Succinate dehydrogenase is the one reaction of the cycle that is linked directly to the electron transport chain and not through the intermediate, NADH. Succinate dehydrogenase is Complex II of the chain and has been described in a previous section. Succinate dehydrogenase is inhibited by oxaloacetate, and the enzyme is in an inhibited state when isolated from the mitochondrion. Whether this plays any role in the regulation of the enzyme is in dispute since the concentration of oxaloacetate in the mitochondrion is so low. However, the concentration required to inhibit the complex is also low, since the enzyme is very sensitive to this intermediate.

Fumarase catalyses a freely reversible reaction in which succinate is hydrated to malate. This enzyme is in concentrations that should not limit the activity of the cycle and hence no control of this reaction is expected or found.

There are two routes for the oxidation of malate in plant mitochondria, that catalysed by malate dehydrogenase which is the same as the animal system and that catalysed by the NAD-specific malic enzyme. It is assumed that under normal mitochondrial activity the flux of carbon is through the malate dehydrogenase. The equilibrium position of this reaction is very much in favour of malate, and so the concentration of malate is normally high in mitochondria as compared with that of oxaloacetate. The rate of the reaction will be determined by the supply of NAD^+ which will be regulated by the activity of the electron transport chain in reoxidizing NADH.

The malic enzyme catalyses the formation of pyruvate from malate with the formation of carbon dioxide and the reduction of NAD^+ to NADH. In this case the reaction is readily reversible. The enzyme has a low affinity for malate and will only operate at high malate concentrations. It has an acid pH optimum and hence under active mitochondrial conditions, when the matrix is expected to be alkaline due to the export of protons from the organelle, the enzyme would be inactive. It may be that, under some conditions, the main flux of carbon into the mitochondrion is via phosphoenolpyruvate carboxylase rather then via pyruvate kinase. This would be one way of supplying pyruvate to the mitochondrial matrix. This could be the case when the mitochondrion is being used for the production of carbon precursors rather than for the formation of ATP.

It has been suggested that the two enzymes that oxidize malate feed electrons into the electron-transport chain through different complexes, one of which bypasses the first coupling site for ATP synthesis. However, there seems to be only one pool of NAD in the mitochondrion and it is difficult to see how this could be achieved. The presence of two complexes is, however, accepted. The non-ATP site may allow metabolites to flow round the cycle even in the presence of high ATP concentrations. It may also be associated with the alternative oxidase to allow oxidation of substrates without formation of ATP at any of the sites.

7.3 The transport of metabolites into the mitochondrion

In addition to its role in producing ATP, the mitochondrion, especially in plants, also synthesizes metabolites for use in the cytosol and oxidizes metabolites other than pyruvate (see Davies, 1979; Douce, 1985; Hanson, 1985). There must, therefore, be a mechanism of interchange between the cytosol and the matrix of the mitochondrion since the inner membrane is impermeable to most compounds. This interchange is facilitated by transport proteins located in the inner membrane (Figure 7.2).

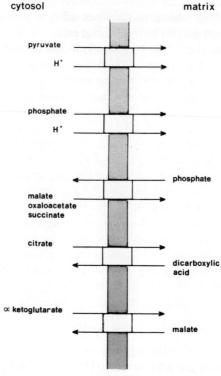

Figure 7.2   The transport of metabolites into and out of the mitochondrion.

The uptake of pyruvate has already been mentioned. This molecule has a specific carrier and the uptake is driven by the proton gradient, so that a proton is taken up as a molecule of pyruvate is transported across the membrane. Hence, the transport is said to be a symport of pyruvate and a proton and the proton gradient is discharged in the process. It has been suggested that under some conditions of high respiration, the uptake of pyruvate may be limiting for the tricarboxylic acid cycle and under these conditions pyruvate is supplied to the matrix by the transport of malate and the action of the malic enzyme.

Phosphate is transported into the mitochondrion by a similar mechanism to pyruvate, that is, it uses a symport with the uptake being driven by the proton gradient. This accumulation of phosphate is essential not only for oxidative phosphorylation but also for the transport of other metabolites into the matrix.

Malate, oxaloacetate and succinate all are taken into the matrix by the same transporter, which is termed the *dicarboxylate transporter*. It appears to be specific for these molecules and does not transport other dicarboxylic acids such as fumarate. The transporter exchanges the dicarboxylates for phosphate, hence the uptake is indirectly linked to the proton gradient via phosphate transport.

Citrate has its own transporter which exchanges a dicarboxylic acid for citrate, the dicarboxylate usually being malate because of its high concentration in the matrix. α-Ketoglutarate is also transported in exchange for malate but this appears to be independent of the citrate transport. Hence, in both these cases the uptake is still driven by the proton gradient via phosphate and malate transport.

Some amino acids are rapidly transported across the inner membrane. There is a carrier that will exchange glutamate for aspartate. This is important because aspartate is rapidly formed in plant cells by transamination of oxaloacetate by glutamate. Aspartate may be transported out of the mitochondrion in exchange for glutamate. Other amino acids such as glycine and serine will penetrate into the matrix, although the mechanism is not known. This exchange is important in photorespiration, as will be described later.

7.4 The interaction of the mitochondrion with the cytosol

There are two features of the transport systems that should be kept in mind. In the first place they are all reversible. Hence, whether a metabolite is transported into or out of the matrix will depend on its internal and external concentration as well as those of the metabolite with which it is exchanged or co-transported. The transporters will therefore simply bring the system to equilibrium and the flux will depend on the metabolic activities of the various cell compartments. In addition, the transport is ultimately dependent upon the proton gradient across the inner membrane; hence the transport depends upon the magnitude of this gradient, which will vary depending on the phosphate potential of the matrix.

The exchange between aspartate and glutamate may be a mechanism to equilibrate reducing equivalents between the cytosol and the matrix. Aspartate is rapidly formed from oxaloacetate in plant cells by trans-amination. Aspartate can therefore be thought of as being equivalent to oxaloacetate. In the cytosol aspartate can be converted to oxaloacetate and then to malate. In this latter reaction cytosolic NADH is converted to NAD^+. Transport of malate into the mitochondrion and its oxidation to oxalocetate generates NADH in the matrix. The oxaloacetate can then be converted back to aspartate. This cycle could, therefore, operate to transport reducing equivalents from the cytosol to the matrix. Conversely, the cycle could operate in reverse and transfer reducing equivalents out of the mitochondrion. This may be used when there is a large requirement for reducing power in the cytosol as for example during the reduction of nitrate to nitrate that occurs in the cytosol and requires NADH.

A major flux of metabolites occurs through the mitochondrion in association with photorespiration and nitrogen metabolism. In both these cases there is a rapid exchange of glutamate, α-ketoglutarate, glycine and serine as will be described later. Although the major site of utilization of these metabolites is the chloroplast and the cytosol, the carbon skeletons are principally made in the mitochondrion.

A major drain on the tricarboxylic acid cycle, in plants especially, is the utilization of succinyl CoA for the synthesis of porphyrins that are required for the synthesis of chlorophylls and the cytochromes. The mitochondrion is the only site of synthesis of succinyl CoA. (See Davies (1979), Douce (1985), Hanson (1985).)

CHAPTER EIGHT

FATTY ACID SYNTHESIS AND BREAKDOWN

8.1 Fatty acid synthesis

8.1.1 Introduction

Fatty acid synthesis is known to occur exclusively in plastids, since it has been shown that the enzymes essential for fatty acid biosynthesis are found only in this organelle (Ohlrogge *et al.*, 1979). Hence, in leaves fatty acids are made in chloroplasts and in seeds they are formed in modified plastids (leucoplasts) that are specialized for fatty acid biosynthesis. The precursor for fatty acid biosynthesis is acetyl CoA. This has first to be activated by the addition of a carboxyl group to the methyl end of the molecule, a process that requires ATP. The product of this reaction, malonyl CoA, then undergoes a series of condensations in which the C_2 unit of the acetyl CoA is converted usually into a C_{18} fatty acid, although shorter chains may be formed in some seeds. The fatty acid is released from the plastid and is further modified by reactions in the cytosol. The modified fatty acid may also re-enter the plastid and form part of the plastid membrane system.

8.1.2 The source of acetyl CoA

It is generally assumed that acetyl CoA cannot cross membranes, so there must be a source of acetyl CoA within the plastid for fatty acid biosynthesis (Dennis and Miernyk, 1982). The principal source of acetyl CoA in the cell arises from the action of the pyruvate dehydrogenase complex in the mitochondrion. In animal cells, this is the only source of acetyl CoA and a mechanism of transporting it across the mitochondrial membrane has evolved. The acetyl CoA is first converted to citrate by citrate synthase. Citrate can traverse the membrane to the cytosol where it is cleaved by citrate lyase, an enzyme that requires ATP, to form acetyl CoA and

D

oxalacetate. Since fatty acid biosynthesis in animals occurs in the cytosol, this acetyl CoA can be used directly. Although citrate lyase has been found in some plants, acetyl CoA in the cytosol is still not available for fatty biosynthesis in the plastid and it is thought that, at least in most cases, this mechanism for transfer of acetyl CoA is not used. It has been suggested that the acetyl CoA in the mitochondrion is first cleaved to acetate that can transverse membranes and that this diffuses to the plastid. It can be converted back to acetyl CoA by an ATP-requiring enzyme, acetyl CoA synthase, which is located in plastids. However, the concentration of free acetate in plant cells is low, so this may be only of minor significance.

It is now generally accepted that acetyl CoA is generated within plastids by a second pyruvate dehydrogenase complex that is quite distinct from the mitochondrial enzyme. This enzyme uses pyruvate that either diffuses into the plastid from the cytosol or is formed within the plastid, through the action of the plastid glycolytic pathway that can convert hexoses into pyruvate. This is particularly important in developing seeds that store oil, where the main function of the plastid is the synthesis of fatty acids. In this case, all the enzymes of the glycolytic pathway have been found in high enough concentration in the leucoplasts to account for the synthesis of fatty acids from hexose without the interaction of any other cell compartment. Whether the same is true for chloroplasts is still an open question, since some of the enzymes of the glycolytic pathway may be absent or in low concentrations in this organelle. In these cases pyruvate may be supplied from the cytosol, or there may be sufficient acetate in the cell for the limited fatty acid biosynthesis that is required by mature leaves.

8.1.3 The formation of malonyl CoA

The first step that is unique to fatty acid biosynthesis is the formation of malonyl CoA catalysed by the enzyme acetyl CoA carboxylase or malonyl CoA synthase. This enzyme is found in plastids and catalyses the following reactions:

$$HCO^{3-} + ATP + biotin \leftrightarrow carboxybiotin + ADP$$

$$carboxybiotin + acetyl\ CoA \leftrightarrow malonyl\ CoA + biotin$$

The enzyme complex consists of three components. A low-molecular-weight protein carries the cofactor of the reaction, biotin, which is attached to the biotin carrier protein through an ε-amino group of a lysine in the protein and hence is on an arm that can swing the biotin between the two enzymes.

The first enzyme of the complex is biotin carboxylase, which carboxy-lates biotin using bicarbonate as the substrate and energy from the hydrolysis of ATP. The biotin carrier protein then moves the carboxybiotin to the second enzyme of the complex, the transcarboxylase, where the carboxyl group attached to the biotin is transferred to the methyl group of the acetyl CoA. Hence, the energy for this reaction comes from the initial hydrolysis of ATP in the first reaction.

The carboxylation of the acetyl CoA is essential to activate the methyl group. The protons of this group are already activated by the CoA group attached to the carboxyl group of the acetate, which results in the lability of the protons. The attachment of the carboxyl group to the methyl group itself further activates the protons, making the methyl group very reactive. Hence, energy derived from the hydrolysis of ATP is used to make the acetyl moiety of the acetyl CoA much more reactive, enabling it to take part in the condensation reactions in the formation of fatty acids. (See Numa and Tanabe (1984), Stumpf (1980; 1984).)

8.1.4 The fatty acid synthetase complex

The fatty acid synthetases from plants and animals, although catalysing identical reactions, are fundamentally different. In plants and bacteria, this enzyme is a complex that can readily be dissociated into its component enzymes, which can be purified and studied independently. In animals, the fatty acid synthetase complex consists of a homodimer of which each monomer is composed of the complete complement of enzymes for fatty acid biosynthesis. These enzymes are part of a single multifunctional protein and hence cannot be separated. See reviews by Alberts and Greenspan (1984); Stumpf (1980, 1984); Wakil *et al.* (1983).

A key component of the fatty acid synthetase in plants is the acyl carrier protein (ACP). This is a low-molecular-weight protein that actually carries the growing fatty acid chain to the various reactions of the synthetase. The functional group of the ACP is identical with that of CoA, and it forms a thioester bond with the acyl group of the fatty acid. The molecular weight of the ACP is around 10 000, and it is readily separated from the synthetase and purified. In contrast, in animals, although the function group of the ACP is identical with that found in plants, it cannot be separated and is an integral part of the synthetase complex.

Antibodies to plant ACP have been raised and used to localize the ACP in plant cells. The only location found is the plastid, i.e. chloroplasts in green leaves and leucoplasts in colourless tisue. Hence, it can be concluded that fatty acid biosynthesis in plants is confined to plastids and does not

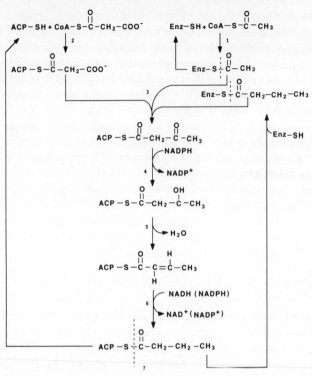

Figure 8.1 The reactions of the fatty acid synthetase complex. The reactions catalysed by this complex are; (1) acetyl transacylase, (2) malonyl transacylase, (3) condensing enzyme, (4) α-keto reductase, (5) dehydratase, (6) enoyl reductase. ACP is acyl carrier protein. This diagram is based on the work of Stumpf and his coworkers.

occur elsewhere in the cell. This has important consequences when one considers the role of fatty acids in the formation of membranes. There must be a complex system of transport of fatty acid into and out of the plastid.

The reactions of the fatty acid synthetase are shown in Figure 8.1. The first reaction can be considered to be the priming reaction of the sequence, and forms the methyl end of the molecule. Acetyle CoA reacts with the ACP of the complex in a reaction that is catalysed by an enzyme called acetyl transacylase. The acetyl group of the acetyle CoA is attached to the ACP through a thioester bond. The acetyl group is then transferred to one of the enzymes of the complex, condensing enzyme, to form a thioester bond with a cysteine group of the enzyme. This frees the —SH of the ACP to form a thioester with malonyl CoA in a reaction catalysed by malonyl transacylase. The next reaction is the essential step in the chain elongation of the fatty acid synthesis. The acetyl group is condensed with the malonyl group attached to the ACP, liberating carbon dioxide and forming a fatty acid four carbons long. This reaction is catalysed by the condensing enzyme, and the energy for this condensation is provided by the decarboxylation of the malonyl group. Ultimately the energy is derived from the carboxylation of acetyl CoA in the acetyl CoA carboxylase reaction.

The next reaction is the first reductive step in fatty acid synthesis. The keto acid is reduced to a β-hydroxy acid, a reaction catalysed by the enzyme β-keto reductase. In animals, the enzyme has an absolute specificity for NADPH as the reductant. In plants NADPH is also the reductant; some plants can use NADH, but only 15% as effectively as NADPH. In the following reaction, the hydroxy acid is dehydrated to form the *trans* unsaturated fatty acid. This is of interest, in that all fatty acids found in the membranes of the cell have a *cis* double bond. The final reaction is the reduction of the unsaturated molecule to the fully saturated fatty acid. This reaction is catalysed by enoyl reductase. In animals it is absolutely specific for NADPH, following the general rule that synthetic reactions use NADPH. Surprisingly, in spinach chloroplasts this reaction is specific for NADH. In other plants there may be both NADH- and NADPH-specific enzymes. In developing oilseeds, where there is excessive fatty acid synthesis for storage lipids, this NADH could be produced by the glycolytic pathway that is present in the plastids of this tissue. In chloroplasts the source of the NADH is less clear. It does, however, represent a large difference between plants and animals.

The above reactions represent one turn of the synthetic cycle in which a C_4 fatty acid is formed. Subsequently, the C_4 acid is transferred to the —SH group of the condensing enzyme, a malonyl group is attached to the ACP and the cycle repeated to form a C_6 fatty acid. By repetition of this cycle a long-chain fatty acid is formed.

The essential reactions for energy metabolism are the reductive steps. Since each NADPH is equivalent to three ATP molecules, or even four if one considers that the $NADP^+/NADPH$ couple is kept 90% reduced, the energy input is very large and amounts to the equivalent of 6 (or 8) ATPs per C_2 unit introduced or a total of 48 (or 64) ATP molecules for a typical C_{18} fatty acid. One must also take into consideration the molecule of ATP that is utilized for the formation of every malonyl CoA molecule. Fatty acids are the main energy store in oilseeds, so it might be assumed that this energy would be made available to the seed on germination. As will be described in the next section, some of the energy available in the fatty acid is, in fact, lost during the oxidation of the fatty acid back to acetyl CoA.

An important regulatory step, which is not well understood, is the means by which the chain length of the fatty acid is controlled. Most plants contain fatty acids that are either sixteen or eighteen carbons in length, but some seeds have fatty acids of chain lengths differing widely from this. It has now been shown that plants contain two condensing enzymes. The first condensing enzyme specifically makes C_{16} fatty acids and has little activity in elongating the C_{16} to C_{18} acids. The second condensing enzyme elongates the C_{16} to C_{18} acids. Hence, the ratio of condensing enzymes is important in determining the ratio of C_{16} to C_{18} in different plants and different tissues. How fatty acids of shorter chain lengths are formed is not known.

Fatty acids are modified in various ways after synthesis of the fully saturated chain. The most common modification is desaturation of the chain. The C_{18} saturated fatty acid stearic acid is desaturated to the C_{16} monounsaturated fatty acid, oleic acid, by means of an enzyme system located in the plastid. This enzyme acts on the ACP derivative of the fatty acids and requires molecular oxygen and NADPH. Plastids are, however, unable to desaturate the fatty acid further and the oleic acid has to be exported. The detailed mechanism of the further desaturation is not known, and the enzymes reponsible have not been isolated.

Fatty acids can be modified in other ways. For example, in the castor oil seed the main storage fatty acid that might account for 90% of the storage fatty acid is ricinoleic acid. This is oleic acid that has been hydroxylated adjacent to the double bond. This hydroxylation occurs in the cytosol and is associated with the endoplasmic reticulum. The function of this modification is not known, although it appears to render the fatty acids indigestible to animals. Many other modifications to fatty acids of this type are known, especially in storage oils.

8.2 The degradation of fatty acids

8.2.1 Introduction

The degradation of fatty acids has been studied mainly in seeds, where there is a massive breakdown of storage lipids during seed germination. However, it can be assumed that there is a constant turnover of membrane phospholipids during the normal metabolism of a cell. Since the breakdown of fatty acids during seed germination occurs only in a specialized organelle called a glyoxysome found only in germinating seeds, this metabolic turnover must occur by some other unknown means. In animals, fatty acid breakdown takes place in the mitochondrion, with the reducing power that is generated being available directly to the electron-transport chain.

A mitochondrial site for fatty acid breakdown has not been demonstrated in plants, although it might occur in the small amount necessary for turnover, which could be below the level that is readily detected. Plants, unlike animals, do not use lipids as a temporary store of energy, which may be one reason for this difference. Lipids are stored in seeds for use only during germination, or in fruits such as the avocado. Plants, however, do have the advantage over animals in that they can convert fatty acids to sugars, whereas animals can only utilize the acetyl CoA *in situ* or transport it as acetyl CoA derivatives such as ketone bodies which serve solely as substrates for the tricarboxylic acid cycle. To maintain blood sugar at acceptable levels, animals must degrade proteins when their reserve polysaccharides are exhausted.

8.2.2 The degradation of storage lipids during seed germination

Oilseeds have recently assumed a major economic importance and are grown on a large scale in many countries throughout the world. Although we are familiar with crop plants that store starch, the major storage material in plants is, in fact, oil. It is generally assumed that oils are stored because they are a very concentrated source of energy, since so much reducing power is used in their formation. However, much of this reducing power is lost during fatty acid breakdown so that the energetic advantages are not as clear as might appear at first.

8.2.3 The degradation of triacylglycerols

The initial step in the breakdown of storage fatty acids is the hydrolysis of the triacylglycerols to free fatty acids and glycerol (Trelease and Doman, 1984). This is catalysed by a lipase located in the membrane of the lipid storage bodies. This enzyme has an acid pH optimum. A second alkaline lipase is located in the glyoxysomes, but this has a much lower activity and probably plays only a minor role. The glycerol that is liberated can be phosphorylated by a glycerol kinase and used directly in the glycolytic pathway. The free fatty acids move to the glyoxysomes by a mechanism that is not at present understood. The concentration of the free acids must be kept low, as they disrupt the activity of the mitochondria.

8.2.4 Fatty acid degradation in the glyoxysome

The only site of fatty acid degradation in the germinating seed is the glyoxysome (Trelease, 1984; Trelease and Doman, 1984). This is an organelle surrounded by a single membrane and characterized by the presence of peroxidase. It is very similar to the peroxisome, and in fact the two organelles may be related. The enzymes of the glyoxysome appear mainly during the early stages of germination. Originally, it was thought that the entire organelle was formed at this time, but more recent evidence indicates that the organelle is present in the ripening seed and that small amounts of the glyoxysomal enzymes are also present at this time. It has been suggested that the large increase of glyoxysome enzyme activity occurring during seed germination is the result of the incorporation of enzymes into the glyoxysomes that persist during seed dehydration.

The mechanism of fatty acid degradation is in some ways the reverse of the synthetic pathway, although the details of the pathway are different and the enzymes and location are not the same. The first step in the pathway is the activation of the free fatty acids to the CoA ester. This is catalysed by the enzyme acyl CoA synthetase, which is located exclusively in the glyoxysomes. Hence, in fatty acid degradation, it is the CoA and not the ACP derivative that is the substrate.

8.2.5 β-Oxidation of fatty acids

Oxidation of fatty acids occurs by a process called β-oxidation (shown in Figure 8.2) because it involves the carbon two atoms removed from the carboxyl carbon of the fatty acid (Alberts and Greenspan, 1984; Bremer and Osmundsen, 1984; Kindl, 1984; Trelease and Doman, 1984). β-Oxidation is catalysed by four enzymes, two of which are located on the same protein molecule, and hence only three proteins are involved. The first reaction is catalysed by an oxidase that removes two hydrogens from the fatty acid; in the process it reduces FAD to $FADH_2$ and forms the *trans* unsaturated fatty acid. The $FADH_2$ is oxidized by molecular

Figure 8.2 The reactions of fatty acid β-oxidation, the glyoxylate cycle and gluconeogenesis, in germinating oil seeds. The enzymes involved in these reactions are (1) acyl-CoA synthetase. (2) acyl-CoA oxidase, (3) catalase, (4) enoyl-CoA hydratase, (5) β-

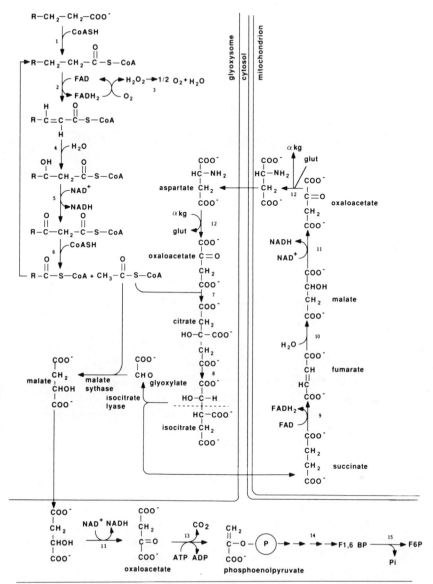

hydroxyacyl-CoA dehydrogenase, (6) β-oxyacyl-CoA thiolase, (7) citrate synthase, (8) aconitase, (9) succinate dehydrogenase, (10) fumarase, (11) malate dehydrogenase, (12) transaminase, (13) phosphoenolpyruvate carboxykinase, (14) reactions of the glycolytic pathway acting in reverse, (15) fructose 1,6-bisphosphatase. The diagram also shows the compartmentation of these pathways and is based on the work of Beevers and his coworkers.

oxygen to form hydrogen peroxide which is broken down by the catalase of the peroxisome to oxygen and water. Hence the reducing power that was trapped during one of the reductive steps of fatty acid synthesis is lost in this step. In animals, where the fatty acid oxidation is in the mitochondrion, this oxidation step is linked directly to the electron-transport chain through ubiquinone so that two ATP molecules can be formed for every fatty acid molecule oxidized. This loss of reducing power during fatty acid oxidation in plants would seem to reduce some of the value of fatty acid storage in seeds.

The next two reactions involve the hydration of the double bond to form the β-hydroxy fatty acid, followed by a dehydrogenation of the hydroxy acid to form the ketoacid. During this later reaction NAD^+ is reduced to NADH. This reducing power is made available for ATP synthesis in the mitochondrion as will be described later. Finally, the ketoacid is cleaved by the enzyme thiolase which releases acetyl-CoA and forms a thioester bond between the remaining fatty acid and free CoA. Hence, a CoA derivative of the fatty acid (which is now two carbons shorter) is released. This fatty acid can undergo the β-oxidation cycle again. By repeated passages through the cycle the fatty acid can be oxidized completely to acetyl-CoA.

8.2.6 The glyoxylate cycle

In animals, the acetyl CoA from fatty acid oxidation is released into the matrix of the mitochondrion where it can be oxidized directly by the tricarboxylic acid cycle. During each turn of this cycle there is a loss of two carbons as carbon dioxide. Hence, during fatty acid oxidation in animals there can be no transfer of carbon from fatty acids to other compounds such as carbohydrates. Under conditions of stress, when blood sugar falls, the animal cannot use stored fats as a source of glucose once reserve polysaccharide is used up. Hence, the animal is forced to mobilize muscle protein, a process that is under hormonal control. Since the ability to convert fatty acids to carbohydrate would appear to be a valuable asset to an animal, it is not clear why this has been lost during evolution since some primitive animals have this ability; it has been reported in some higher animals, but only at a particular stage of development.

In germinating seeds the two oxidative steps of the tricarboxylic acid cycle are avoided by the reactions of the glyoxylate cycle (Figure 8.2) that occur in the glyoxysome (Beevers, 1978; 1979; 1980; Mettler and Beevers, 1980). Some of the reactions of this cycle are catalysed by enzymes that have an identical function to enzymes found in the mitochondrion. The catalysts are, however, distinct proteins, and are, therefore, isozymes of the mitochondrial enzymes. The first reaction of the cycle is the condensation of the acetyl CoA from the fatty oxidation with oxaloacetate to form citrate, a reaction catalysed by citrate synthase. This is then converted to isocitrate by aconitase. The next two reactions are unique to the glyoxylate cycle, and are found only in the glyoxysome. It is these reactions that allow the oxidative steps of the tricarboxylic acid cycle to be bypassed.

The first reaction is catalysed by isocitrate lyase which cleaves isocitrate to glyoxylate and succinate. The glyoxylate generated in the glyoxysome by isocitrate lyase is condensed with a second molecule of acetyl CoA to form malate. This reaction is catalysed by malate synthase, the second enzyme unique to this cycle. This malate can be considered to be the end product of the glyoxylate cycle, since it is exported from the glyoxysome to the cytosol where it is converted to hexose phosphate. These reactions of the cycle do not involve any loss of carbon as carbon dioxide.

The succinate generated by the isocitrate lyase reaction is now transported to the mitochondrion, where it is converted by the reactions of the tricarboxylic acid cycle to oxaloacetate. The oxaloacetate moves back to the glyoxysome and re-enters the glyoxylate cycle. Hence, the glyoxylate cycle involves the cycling of metabolites between the glyoxysome and the mitochondrion; in the process, malate is exported to the cytosol. Since two molecules of acetyl CoA enter the cycle from fatty acid breakdown, in effect, the two acetyl groups are the source of malate. This is accomplished without the loss of carbon as carbon dioxide.

One problem that should be discussed is the fate of the reducing power generated in the form of NADH during fatty acid oxidation and the operation of the glyoxylate cycle. It is assumed that this NADH is converted back to NAD^+ by transporting the reducing power to the mitochondrion. How this is achieved has not been determined with any certainty. It is unlikely that NADH itself is transferred, as it does not readily cross membranes. It is more likely that a shuttle system exists in which malate from the glyoxysome is transported to the mitochondrion where it is converted to oxaloacetate by malate dehydrogenase, generating NADH. The oxaloacetate is probably transaminated to aspartate which can be transported back to the glyoxysome where it is reconverted to oxaloacetic acid. In the presence of excess NADH the oxaloacetate will be reduced to malate, completing the cycle. The effect of this cycle is to transfer NADH from the glyoxysome to the mitochondrion for oxidation.

The gluconeogenic pathway is the final sequence for the conversion of fatty acids to hexose phosphates which can be utilized for sucrose biosynthesis. The oxalacetate is converted by the enzyme phosphoenol-pyruvate carboxykinase to PEP. This reaction involves the only release of carbon dioxide in the entire sequence from fatty acid to hexose. It also requires the hydrolysis of ATP, as shown below:

$$ATP + oxaloacetate \leftrightarrow ADP + CO_2 + PEP$$

The PEP can then be converted to fructose 1,6-bisphosphate by the reversal of the glycolytic pathway, a process that occurs in the cytosol of the cell. Finally, the fructose 1,6-bisphosphate is converted to fructose 6-phosphate by the enzyme fructose 1,6-bisphosphatase which releases inorganic phosphate. This bypasses the unfavourable equilibrium of the phosphofructokinase reaction.

As discussed earlier, the glycolytic pathway consists of a series of pools connected by steps that are basically irreversible. Whether the pathway moves in the direction of glycolysis will depend on the input of metabolites into the various pools. Clearly, some of the steps must be highly regulated; these have been shown to be primarily the interconversion of fructose 6-phosphate and fructose 1,6-bisphosphate and the conversion of phos-phoenolpyruvate to pyruvate. These steps are not at equilibrium, and hence must be under tight metabolic control. Without this control there would be a futile loss of ATP as metabolites cycled between the glycolytic and gluconeogenic reactions.

Hence plants have the ability, not present in higher animals, to convert fatty acids into hexoses. This involves three cell compartments, and again emphasizes the importance of compartmentation in plant cell metabolism.

CHAPTER NINE

THE CARBON REDUCTION CYCLE

9.1 Introduction

The carbon reduction cycle is normally dealt with in textbooks as a single phenomenon (for example Bidwell, 1983; Gregory, 1978; Robinson and Walker, 1981). It is important, however, to realize that it consists of three distinct steps. First, inorganic carbon dioxide is fixed into an organic molecule that can then be reduced in the second step. Finally, the reduced carbon can be utilized either to regenerate the carbon dioxide acceptor molecule or for other functions in the cell. Originally, it was thought that sucrose was synthesized in the chloroplast and then exported to the cytosol. It is now known that sucrose is synthesized in the cytosol from carbon supplied as triose phosphate from the chloroplast. It must, however, be remembered that plastids, including chloroplasts, are a major site of biosynthetic reactions in the cell. Some of the intermediates of the carbon reduction cycle other than triose may be used in these reactions so that the drain of carbon from the cycle may occur at a number of places.

9.2 The fixing of carbon dioxide: ribulose bisphosphate carboxylase (RuBPcase)

Ribulose bisphosphate carboxylase (RuBPcase) is the most abundant protein in the world and may constitute up to 50% of the soluble protein in a leaf. It is often described as ribulose bisphosphate carboxylase/oxygenase, but enzymologically speaking the oxygenase function is trivial and the enzyme is, in fact, a highly specialized carboxylase. In practice, because the concentration of oxygen in the atmosphere is approximately 1000 times higher than that of carbon dioxide, the oxygenase function presents problems for the metabolism of the plant that have been overcome in various ways. The enzyme is an octamer and is composed of eight

CARBOXYLASE

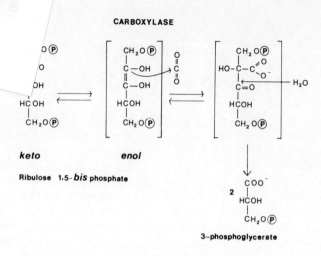

OXYGENASE

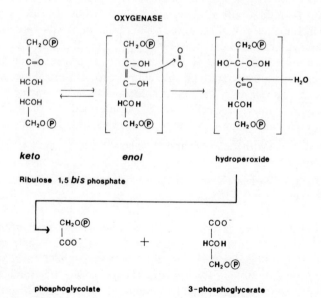

Figure 9.1 The carboxylase and oxygenase reactions of ribulose 1,5-bisphosphate carboxylase. Based on the work described by Lorimer and co-workers.

large and eight small subunits. The large subunits are encoded in the chloroplast DNA, whereas the small subunits are encoded in the nuclear genome, translated in the cytosol and imported into the chloroplast, where the complex enzyme is assembled. The active site of the enzyme is on the large subunit, but the small subunit is also required for activity.

RuBPcase catalyses the carboxylation of ribulose 1,5-bisphosphate (see Lorimer (1981), Lorimer and Andrews (1981), Miziorko and Lorimer (1983)) by the reaction shown in Figure 9.1. The first step in the reaction is the binding of RuBP to the active site of the enzyme. This causes a rearrangement of the RuBP from the keto form of the sugar to the enol form. The extraction of a proton from the —OH of carbon 3 of the molecule and the subsequent rearrangement leaves a negative charge on carbon 2 that can be attacked by the positive charge on the carbon atom of carbon dioxide with the formation of a carboxyl group attached to carbon 2. This six-carbon intermediate, which is not released from the enzyme, is rapidly hydrolysed to form two molecules of 3-phosphogly-cerate. Although there are internal oxidation–reduction reactions within the molecules of this reaction, there is no overall reduction of the RuBP or the carbon dioxide. This reaction simply fixes the carbon dioxide into two organic molecules that are reduced at a later stage. The free energy change of the reaction is $-33\,kJ/mol$, under the conditions found in the cell, so the reaction is very much in favour of carboxylation.

For many years, problems were thought to exist with this enzyme because the affinity for its substrate appeared to be too low for the enzyme to function effectively at atmospheric concentrations of carbon dioxide. However, it was discovered that, if the enzyme was very rapidly isolated from active photosynthetic tissue and assayed immediately, it had a much higher affinity for carbon dioxide, and in this form would have sufficient activity at atmospheric carbon dioxide concentrations to catalyse carbon dioxide fixation at a rate occurring *in vivo*.

RuBPcase is now known to exist in an active and an inactive state. The conversion of one state to the other is very slow relative to the rate of catalysis. On isolation, the inactive form predominates unless the enzyme is assayed rapidly, and this was the source of the problems that were originally attributed to the enzyme. It has now been shown that RuBPcase can be activated by incubating the enzyme with carbon dioxide and magnesium. This is a slow reaction, and involves the binding of the carbon dioxide at a site that is quite distinct from the active site. After the carbon dioxide is bound, the enzyme displays the kinetics that one might expect of an enzyme that is essential for photosynthesis.

9.3 The reduction of 3-phosphoglycerate

The reduction of 3-phosphoglycerate occurs by two reactions that are essentially the reverse of the reactions involved in the oxidation of glyceraldehyde 3-phosphate in glycolysis. The photosynthetic reactions, however, take place in the chloroplast rather than the cytosol, they are catalysed by distinct enzymes, and the reductive step uses NADPH instead of NADH.

The phosphorylation of 3-phosphoglycerate is catalysed by the chloroplast isozyme of 3-phosphoglycerate kinase. The equilibrium position of this reaction favours 3-phosphoglycerate and, consequently, 3-phosphoglycerate is often found at high concentrations in plant tissues. In order for 1,3-bisphosphoglycerate to be formed, the concentration of ATP relative to ADP must be high; a condition that will be found during photosynthesis. In addition, 1,3-bisphosphoglycerate must be removed; this is accomplished by the second enzyme, glyceraldehyde 3-phosphate dehydrogenase.

The reaction catalysed by the glyceraldehyde 3-phosphate dehydrogenase is specific for NADP, and is a completely separate enzyme from the NAD-specific enzyme that is found in the cytosolic glycolytic pathway. An NAD-specific enzyme is often found in chloroplasts and can be at high concentrations in non-photosynthetic plastids, but this is a separate enzyme and is not involved in photosynthesis. This reaction is reversible. However, in the light, the concentration of NADPH relative to $NADP^+$ is very high, and this will push the reaction in favour of glyceraldehyde 3-phosphate. Hence, because of the high ATP and NADPH concentrations during photosynthesis the formation of the trioses is favoured. Glyceraldehyde 3-phosphate dehydrogenase is light-activated by reduction, the electrons being ultimately derived from the electron transport chain. This activation system acts through an intermediate called thioredoxin, as will be described later.

These are the two crucial reactions of photosynthesis, since two molecules of 3-phosphoglycerate formed by the fixation of one molecule of carbon dioxide are reduced to the level of carbohydrate. In effect, one molecule of carbon dioxide is reduced to the carbohydrate level in a process that requires four electrons and two molecules of ATP. Hence, the energy requirements for this process are very large. Triose phosphate can be considered to be the end-product of photosynthesis, since it is the compound that is exported to the cytosol. Alternatively, it can either be utilized in the chloroplast for starch synthesis and the other biosynthetic reactions or cycled to regenerate ribulose 1,5-bisphosphate to serve as the acceptor for additional carbon dioxide molecules.

9.4 The regeneration of the acceptor molecule: ribulose 1,5-bisphosphate

One of the early triumphs of the use of isotopes in biology was the elucidation of the flow of carbon from carbon dioxide into the sugars that are found in the chloroplast (see Bidwell, 1983; Gregory, 1978; Robinson and Walker, 1981). This cycle is now called the reductive pentose phosphate pathway (although it may still be referred to as the Calvin cycle). As its name suggests, the cycle is very similar to the oxidative pentose phosphate pathway and many of the reactions are in fact identical. However, in the oxidative pathway the cycle starts with two oxidative steps whereas in the reductive pathway the cycle starts with the reductive step described above. The reactions of the pathway, which are similar but not identical to the reversible reactions of the oxidative pentose phosphate cycle, are shown in Figure 9.2.

The basic function of the pathway is to convert glyceraldehyde 3-phosphate into ribulose 5-phosphate. In effect, five trioses are converted into three pentoses. The enzymes catalysing these reactions are isozymes of the enzymes that catalyse the reversible reactions of the oxidative pathway in the cytosol. Hence, glyceraldehyde 3-phosphate is converted to dihydroxyacetone phosphate by triose phosphate isomerase. The two trioses then undergo an aldol condensation catalysed by aldolase to form fructose 1,6-bisphosphate. This is converted by a specific phosphatase into fructose 6-phosphate with the release of inorganic phosphate. This reaction, therefore, bypasses the energetically unfavourable step of phosphofructokinase. The phosphatase is highly regulated, and is active only under photosynthetic conditions. The activation appears to be under the control of thioredoxin. The enzyme itself is active in the reduced state when photosynthetic reducing power is available. The inactivation in the dark prevents the breakdown of fructose 1,6-bisphosphate produced by the chloroplastic phosphofructokinase. This enzyme is active in the dark and catalyses the breakdown of stored starch in the chloroplast. The requirement of light for the activation of the fructose 1,6-bisphosphate phosphatase prevents the formation of a futile cycle between fructose 6-phosphate and fructose 1,6-bisphosphate in the dark which would simply result in the destruction of ATP.

The rest of the reactions of the cycle are involved in a rearrangement of the carbon atoms in fructose 6-phosphate, glyceraldehyde 3-phosphate and

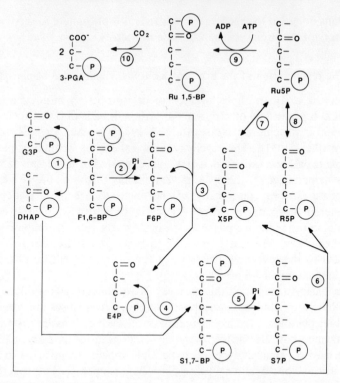

Figure 9.2 The reactions of the reductive pentose phosphate pathway. To simplify the diagram, only the carbon backbone of the sugars is shown. The hydroxyl groups are indicated by single lines and the keto or aldehyde functions by a double-bonded oxygen. The abbreviations used are; G3P, glyceraldehyde 3-phosphate; DHAP, dihydroxyacetone phosphate; Fl,6BP, fructose 1,6-bisphosphate; F6P, fructose 6-phosphate; E4P, erythrose 4-phosphate; X5P, xylulose 5-phosphate; R5P, ribose 5-phosphate; S1,7BP, sedoheptulose 1,7-biphosphate; S7P, sedoheptulose 7-phosphate; Ru5P, ribulose 5-phosphate; Rul,5BP, ribulose 1,5-bisphosphate; 3PGA, 3-phosphoglycerate. The enzymes catalysing the reactions are: (1) aldolase, (2) fructose 1,6 bisphosphatase, (3) transketolase, (4) aldolase, (5) sedoheptulose 1,7-bisphophatase, (6) transketolase, (7) ribulose 5-phosphate 3-epimerase, (8) ribose 5-phosphate isomerase, (9) ribulose 5-phosphate kinase, (10) ribulose 1,5-bisphosphate carboxylase.

dihydroxyacetone phosphate into the pentose, ribulose 5-phosphate. These reactions (numbered according to Figure 9.2) are catalysed by: (3) trans-ketolase which forms erythrose 4-phosphate and xylulose 5-phosphate from fructose 6-phosphate and glyceraldehyde 3-phosphate (4) aldolase which forms sedoheptulose 1,7-bisphosphate from erythrose 4-phosphate and dihydroxyacetone phosphate (this may be the same aldolase that is involved in the formation of fructose 1,6-bisphosphate), (5)-sedo-heptulose 1,7-bisphosphate phosphatase (this may be the same enzyme that removes the phosphate from fructose 1;6-bisphosphate and is activated in a similar fashion to that enzyme), (6) transketolase which forms xylulose 5-phosphate and ribose 5-phosphate from sedoheptulose 7-phosphate and glyceraldehyde 3-phosphate (this is the same enzyme that catalysed reaction (3), (7) ribulose 5-phosphate 3-epimerase which forms ribulose 5-phosphate from xylulose 5-phosphate, (8) ribose 5-phosphate isomerase which forms ribulose 5-phosphate from ribose 5-phosphate. All these reactions are reversible, apart from the phosphatases.

The final reaction of the cycle is the conversion of ribulose 5-phosphate to ribulose 1,5-bisphosphate. This reaction is catalysed by ribulose 5-phosphate kinase and constitutes the second step in the reductive pentose phosphate pathway where ATP is required. The equilibrium position of the reaction is in favour of the ribulose 1,5-bisphosphate. This enzyme is again activated by light via the electron-transport chain and thioredoxin.

Overall, in the fixation of one molecule of carbon dioxide and its reduction to the carbohydrate level, two molecules of NADPH and three molecules of ATP are required. It has been suggested that this imbalance of reducing equivalents and ATP is the reason that cyclic photophosphorylation is required. This would enable the extra ATP to be synthesized in the presence of adequate NADPH to ensure that the above stoichiometry is maintained.

9.5 The control of the reductive pentose phosphate cycle

The most straightforward control of the cycle is the supply of ATP and NADPH. These molecules are rapidly turned over in the chloroplast. In the dark the NADPH will be oxidized to $NADP^+$, and similarly the ATP/ADP ratio will fall. Together this will prevent the conversion of 3-phosphoglycerate to glyceraldehyde 3-phosphate. The reaction catalysed by ribulose 5-phosphate kinase is also controlled by the ATP/ADP ratio, and this reaction will also be inhibited.

A second effect is a direct result of chloroplast metabolism in the light. In the light, protons are pumped into the thylakoid vesicles. This results in an increase of the pH of the stroma by as much as one pH unit from a pH of 7 to a pH of 8. Many of the enzymes involved in photosynthesis have alkaline pH optima, and the increase in pH of the stroma has a profound effect on their activity. In addition, as protons are pumped into the thylakoids magnesium ions are pumped out so that the magnesium ion concentration may rise by as much as five-fold. Many of the chloroplast enzymes require high magnesium ion concentrations for activity.

There is a direct activation of some enzymes of the cycle by the photosynthetic apparatus of the chloroplast (Buchanan, 1980; Buchanan *et al.*, 1979). *In vitro* four enzymes of the cycle, glyceraldehyde 3-phosphate dehydrogenase, fructose 1,6-bisphosphatase, sedoheptulose 1,7-bisphosphatase and ribulose 5-phosphate kinase can be activated by reducing agents. These enzymes are less active in their oxidized state and increase in activity upon reduction. This reduction is linked directly to the electron-transport chain, probably through ferredoxin. Hence, when ferredoxin is reduced these four enzymes become reduced and are activated. There is, therefore, a direct link between the redox state of the electron-transport chain and the activity of the enzymes resulting in a coordinated control of chloroplast metabolism.

Two mechanisms for the link between the electron transport chain and the enzymes have been proposed. A small protein has been isolated that will facilitate the reduction of these enzymes by artificial reductants. This protein has been termed thioredoxin, and is reduced by an enzyme called thioredoxin reductase that links it to ferredoxin and consequently to the electron transport chain. In a second mechanism that has been proposed, termed the light effect mediator system or LEM, the components are membrane-bound and interact directly with the electron transport chain. In both cases, it has been proposed that disulphide groups in the enzyme are reduced and the enzyme becomes activated or inhibited by light through the action of the electron transport chain.

The final method of control is directly linked to the requirement of metabolites by the cell. The pool of metabolites in the stroma of the chloroplast is in equilibrium with that of the cytosol through the phosphate translocator in the inner membrane of the chloroplast. The activity of this translocator equilibrates triose phosphates, 3-phosphoglycerate and inorganic phosphate across the membrane. The cytosolic and stromal interaction will be discussed in more detail later.

CHAPTER TEN

PHOTORESPIRATION

10.1 Introduction

Photorespiration was a term coined some years ago (see Bidwell, 1983) to distinguish a form of carbon dioxide evolution in leaves, occurring in the light, that differs from normal respiration and is not related to the activity of glycolysis and the tricarboxylic acid cycle. It was found that if leaves that had been actively photosynthesizing were rapidly placed in the dark, and the carbon dioxide exchange monitored, there was a burst of carbon dioxide evolution from the leaves immediately on darkening. This was assumed to be a remnant of a respiratory process that was occurring in the light, which could not be detected because of the massive uptake of carbon dioxide during photosynthesis. Photorespiration, and the source of this carbon dioxide, was a mystery for a number of years and it is only recently that the mechanism has been elucidated in any detail.

10.2 The oxygenase activity of ribulose bisphosphate carboxylase (RuBPcase)

It has been indicated previously that ribulose bisphosphate carboxylase (RuBPcase) has a high affinity for carbon dioxide compared with its affinity for oxygen. Hence, it will preferentially bind carbon dioxide. However, even highly specific enzymes will bind other competing molecules if they are present at very high concentrations. It appears that, during evolution, the affinity for carbon dioxide compared with that for oxygen has been increased to the maximum, since carboxylases from all sources react with oxygen to about the same extent. This high specificity for carbon dioxide is essential, considering the ratio of oxygen to carbon dioxide in the atmosphere. (See reviews by Lorimer, 1981; Lorimer and Andrews, 1981; Miziorko and Lorimer, 1983.)

In fact, it now appears that there is no binding site for oxygen; the oxygen simply reacts with the ribulose 1,5-bisphosphate on the surface of the enzyme. The oxygenase activity can be suppressed by lowering the oxygen content in the atmosphere in which the plants are grown to 2% instead of the atmospheric concentration of 20%. Under these conditions the yield of photosynthate is increased. From this, it has been argued that the oxygenase activity of the carboxylase is a wasteful reaction, and that if it could be suppressed, the yields of crop plants could be significantly increased. This has resulted in a great deal of research on photorespiration.

The exact mechanism of the attack of oxygen on the ribulose bisphosphate has not been elucidated. As described earlier, there is a keto to enol transformation of the substrate on the enzyme surface. It is postulated that there is then an extraction of a proton from carbon 3 to leave a nucleophilic centre at carbon 2. This centre can be attacked by a carbon dioxide molecule in the normal carboxylation reaction or by oxygen in the oxygenase reaction. This attack by oxygen probably results in the formation of a peroxide radical that can be hydrolysed to give one molecule of phosphoglycolate and one molecule of 3-phosphoglycerate. In this reaction, therefore, no carbon dioxide is fixed.

The phosphoglycolate is rapidly removed by a phosphatase that cleaves off the phosphate group to form glycolate and inorganic phosphate. Mutants lacking this enzyme can be grown in 2% oxygen when the oxygenase activity of RuBPcase is inhibited, but rapidly die when exposed to air because of the accumulation of phosphoglycolate. The glycolate liberated by the phosphatase reaction is recycled back to the chloroplast by the reactions of the glycolate pathway (Figure 10.1). This pathway, therefore, acts as a mechanism for salvaging the carbon of phosphoglycolate and returning it to the reductive pentose phosphate pathway. Without the glycolate pathway, this carbon would be lost and photosynthesis inhibited by the inability to regenerate ribulose 1,5-bisphosphate.

In the glycolate pathway (Beevers, 1979; Bidwell, 1983; Tolbert 1981), two molecules of glycolate are converted to one molecule of phosphoglyceric acid and one molecule of carbon dioxide. In Figure 10.1 the first part of the pathway is doubled to account for this stoichiometry. Glycolate is released from the chloroplast and diffuses to the peroxisome where it is oxidized to glyoxylate by glycolate oxidase using oxygen as the electron acceptor. The glyoxylate is then transaminated to form glycine. As will be described later, two molecules of glycine are required in the next reactions of this cycle. The amino donor for the formation of one of glycine molecules is glutamate that is formed in the chloroplast; the deaminated

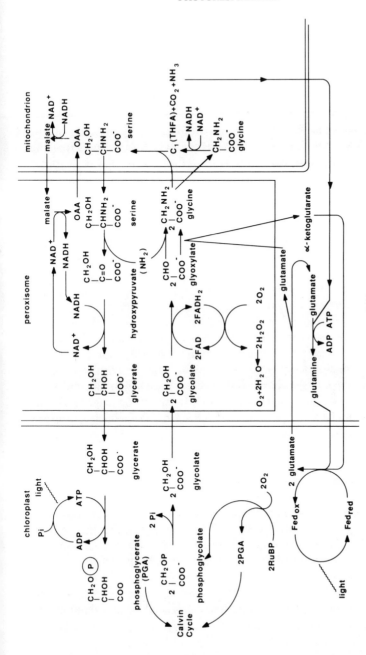

Figure 10.1 The glycolate pathway for the conversion of phosphoglycolate to 3-phosphoglycerate. The initial reactions of the pathway are shown doubled because two molecules of phosphoglycolate are required for every molecule of phosphoglycerate that is produced. The abbreviations used in this diagram are: Fed$_{red}$, Fed$_{ox}$, the reduced and oxidized forms of ferredoxin; **RuBP**, ribulose 1,5-bisphosphate; PGA, 3-phosphoglycerate; THFA, tetrahydrofolic acid; OAA, oxaloacetate. This diagram is based on the work of Tolbert and his co-workers.

product is α-ketoglutarate. The second amino donor is serine, whose formation is described below.

The glycine migrates to the mitochondrion where it undergoes a complex reaction in which two molecules of glycine are used to form one molecule of serine (see Douce, 1985). This conversion involves two enzymes. In the first reaction, catalysed by glycine decarboxylase, one of the glycine molecules is oxidized to carbon dioxide, ammonia and a C_1 unit attached to a carrier molecule known as tetrahydrofolate. In the process of this oxidation, NAD^+ is reduced to NADH. It is in this reaction that the carbon dioxide of photorespiration is lost. The second enzyme involved in the formation of serine is serine hydroxymethyl transferase, which adds the C_1 unit from the tetrahydrofolate to a second glycine molecule with the formation of serine. This enzyme has not been characterized in any detail from plant cells.

The serine is exported from the mitochondrion back to the peroxisome where it is deaminated by a transaminase reaction to form hydroxypyruvate. The amino group is transferred to one of the glyoxylate molecules, as described above. Hence, the two molecules of glycine in the first part of the pathway are formed by two different amino transfer reactions. The hydroxypyruvate produced by the transamination reaction is then reduced to glycerate by the enzyme hydroxypyruvate reductase using NADH as the reductant. The NADH for this reduction is derived from the mito-chondrion by the shuttle system shown in Figure 10.1. Finally the glycerate is transported back to the chloroplast, where it is phosphorylated to form 3-phosphoglycerate by a kinase using ATP from photophosphorylation. This 3-phosphoglycerate can then be utilized by the reductive pentose phosphate cycle.

10.3 The function of photorespiration

Many functions have been proposed for photorespiration, and there are still adherents to most of them (see Bidwell, 1983). The simplest explan-ation is that the high concentration of oxygen in the atmosphere, relative to that of carbon dioxide, makes the oxygenase activity of the ribulose 1,5-bisphosphate carboxylase unavoidable, and results in the formation of phosphoglycolate. This, in turn, creates a problem. The loss of carbon from the reductive pentose phosphate pathway will lead to an inhibition of photosynthesis because of a reduction in the recycling of trioses to the carbon dioxide acceptor molecule, ribulose bisphosphate. The glycolate cycle, therefore, operates to salvage this carbon from phosphoglycolate and return it to the reductive pentose phosphate cycle as phosphoglycerate.

At one time, it was thought that if the photorespiration could be inhibited, then the productivity of crop plants could be increased. This is correct, since decreasing the oxygenase activity of RuBPcase by growing plants in 2% oxygen does increase yield. This approach, however, cannot be extended to the glycolate cycle, since inhibition of this cycle is injurious to the plant. This has been elegantly shown by the work of Sommerville, who has developed mutants of a small plant called *Arabidopsis* that lack various enzymes of the glycolate pathway. Under respiratory conditions, all these mutations are lethal and the plants can only survive in low concentrations of oxygen. This shows that the pathway is not an anomaly but an essential feature for life in an atmosphere that contains 20% oxygen.

10.4 The requirement for three organelles in the pathway

One of the mysteries of the glycolate pathway is that it is very complex and involves three organelles. One can only assume that during evolution no simpler method of converting phosphoglycolate back to 3-phosphoglycerate has been developed. There are some speculations that could be made regarding the utilization of the various organelles. Glycine decarboxylase is found in the mitochondria of animals as well as plants. This location of the enzyme means that there is a transfer of reducing power from the chloroplast to the mitochondrion. This reducing power could be used for mitochondrial ATP synthesis or it could be exported to the cytosol. However, the reduction of hydroxypyruvate requires NADH. This NADH is transported from the mitochondrion by the shuttle system shown in Figure 10.1. Hence, all the NADH formed by the decarboxylation of glycine is used in the peroxisome, and there will be no excess if the pathway is operating completely.

The involvement of the peroxisome is more difficult to rationalize. The glycolate oxidase reaction releases hydrogen peroxide, a highly toxic material in the cell. Peroxisomes contain high concentrations of catalase which will rapidly remove this compound. The location of the oxidase and the catalase in the same compartment would therefore facilitate this step. The use of an oxidase in this reaction would make it irreversible; this may be the reason for the evolution of an oxidase in place of a dehydrogenase which would conserve the reducing power. In algae, however, a dehydro-genase is in fact used.

10.5 The importance of nitrogen metabolism in photorespiration

There are two further problems in the glycolate pathway that have to be overcome if the pathway is to be maintained. Both of these involve nitrogen metabolism, and require a cycling of amino compounds and ammonia, in addition to the complex flux of carbon (see Bidwell, 1983; Douce, 1985). In the reaction catalysed by glycine decarboxylase, ammonia is liberated. This ammonia is highly mobile and permeable to cell membranes. If it is lost from the cell, the cycle will come to a halt, as the formation of glycine in the peroxisome is catalysed by two transaminases which require amino donors.

The ammonia released by glycine decarboxylase is re-assimilated into glutamate by two reactions. In the cytosol, or the chloroplast in some plants, the ammonia is first assimilated by a reaction catalysed by glutamine synthase, in which glutamine is formed from ammonia and glutamate. This reaction requires ATP. The second reaction occurs in the chloroplast and is catalysed by glutamate synthetase. In this reaction, the amide group from the glutamine is transferred to α-ketoglutarate with the formation of two molecules of glutamate. This reaction requires reducing power which is supplied as reduced ferredoxin from the electron-transport chain. These two reactions have a large energy requirement, since one requires ATP and the other two electrons from ferredoxin, or the equivalent of one molecule of NADPH.

The second problem faced by the glycolate cycle is the imbalance of transamination reactions in the peroxisome. Two molecules of glyoxylate are transaminated to glycine for every molecule of serine that is deaminated to hydroxypyruvate. Hence, a second amino donor must be imported into the peroxisome. This second amino donor is glutamate formed by the assimilation of ammonia by the reactions of glutamine synthase and glutamate synthetase. Hence, this ammonia ultimately comes from the decarboxylation of glycine in the mitochondrion.

It is clear that there is not only a complex flux of carbon in photo-respiration, but an equally complex shuttling of ammonia and amino compounds. It has been calculated that the amount of ammonia assimil-ated during photorespiration is at least twenty times that required for normal cell growth. Mutants with low levels of glutamate synthetase can survive when grown under 2% oxygen because the amount of glutamate synthase they contain is sufficient for cell growth. However, these mutants die under photorespiratory conditions because of their inability to assimilate the ammonia released during the decarboxylation of glycine. The cell dies because the formation of glycine in the peroxisome is inhibited by the lack of amino donors; hence the glycolate pathway cannot operate.

CHAPTER ELEVEN

THE AVOIDANCE OF PHOTORESPIRATION: THE C_4 PLANTS

11.1 Introduction

In photorespiration, there is a net loss to the plant, not only of carbon dioxide, but also of energy in the form of reducing power. This loss of reduced carbon occurs in the glycolate oxidase step in the glycolate pathway where electrons are passed to oxygen. If plants could avoid this loss, they would be more efficient and more competitive. It appears that modification of the RuBPcase, so that it loses its oxygenase activity, is not possible. Attempts at inhibiting the glycolate pathway cause the death of the plant; this pathway is therefore also essential and cannot be eliminated. However, oxygen and carbon dioxide are competitive at the active site of the carboxylase, and photorespiration could be reduced if the concentration of carbon dioxide could be raised relative to that of oxygen. It is this strategy that has been adopted by the C_4 plants (see Bidwell, 1983; Edwards and Huber, 1981; Gardestrom and Edwards, 1985).

11.2 The structure of C_4 plants

An essential feature of all C_4 plants, of which there are three types, appears to be the requirement for two distinct tissues. The function of one of these tissues is to collect carbon dioxide, which is then transported to the second tissue where it is concentrated and fixed by RuBP case. It is because of the high concentration of carbon dioxide at the active site of the carboxylase that photorespiration is avoided. Surrounding the vascular bundles in the C_4 plants are specialized cells, termed bundle sheath or Kranz cells, after the researcher who first described their structure. These cells are circular in section. Their most notable feature when seen in the electron microscope is the absence or reduction of the grana in the chloroplasts. The rest of the leaf structure, the mesophyll, is occupied by more elongated cells which have a chloroplast structure that is typical of higher plant chloroplasts in having well-defined grana. The most interesting feature of this Kranz type of leaf structure is that it is found in quite different genera of plants and seems to have arisen independently a number of times during evolution. In all cases, Kranz anatomy appears to be a prerequisite for C_4 biochemistry.

11.3 The biochemistry of C_4 plants

The essential difference in the biochemistry of C_4 plants (Edwards and Huber, 1981; Ogren, 1984) becomes evident when they are fed radioactive carbon dioxide. The first labelled compounds that are detected are C_4 acids, in contrast with the three-carbon compound, phosphoglycerate, of C_3 plants (Figure 11.1). The initial reaction in carbon fixation occurs in the mesophyll cells and is catalysed by the enzyme phosphoenolpyruvate carboxylase, which catalyses the following reaction:

$$phosphoenolpyruvate + HCO^{3-} + H_2O \leftrightarrow oxaloacetate + Pi$$

The active carbon species that is fixed is the bicarbonate ion, instead of carbon dioxide, as was the case for the RuBPcase. The affinity of the enzyme for bicarbonate is very high, which enables very low concentrations of carbon dioxide to be used.

The oxaloacetate formed, in this reaction, is reduced to malate by the enzyme malate dehydrogenase which used NADPH as the reductant. This enzyme is located in the chloroplast, and hence the oxaloacetate that is formed in the cytosol has to be transported into the chloroplast. Recently, a carrier has been detected in these chloroplasts that is specific for oxaloacetate. The NADP malate dehydrogenase is light-activated by a specific thioredoxin system distinct from that described previously for the activation of the enzymes of the reductive pentose phosphate pathway. The malate that is formed in the mesophyll cells of the leaf then diffuses to the bundle sheath cells, probably down a large concentration gradient between these cells.

Within the bundle sheath cell, the malate is decarboxylated in the chloroplast by an NADP-specific malic enzyme that decarboxylates malate with the formation of carbon dioxide, NADPH and pyruvate:

$$malate + NADP^+ \leftrightarrow CO_2 + pyruvate + NADPH + H^+$$

The carbon dioxide fixed in the mesophyll cells as malate is, therefore,

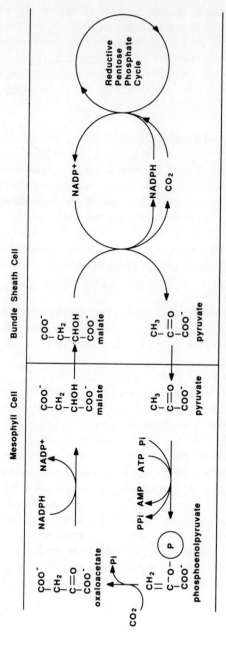

Figure 11.1 The movement of metabolites between the mesophyll and bundle sheath cells in one type of C_4 plant. Based on the work of Hatch and Slack and their co-workers.

released in the chloroplast of the bundle sheath. The high concentration of carbon dioxide in these chloroplasts can compete with oxygen to prevent the oxygenase activity of RuBPcase. Not only carbon dioxide is delivered to the bundle sheath chloroplasts, but also NADPH formed during the reaction of the malic enzyme. Within the bundle sheath cells, the carbon dioxide is fixed by RuBPcase and is reduced by the regular reductive pentose phosphate pathway using the NADPH formed by the decarboxylation of malate by the malic enzyme.

The pyruvate formed in this reaction diffuses back down a concentration gradient to the mesophyll cells. In order for carbon dioxide fixation to continue, this pyruvate must be converted back to the carbon dioxide acceptor molecule, PEP (see Edwards *et al.*, 1985). This occurs by a quite remarkable reaction catalysed by the enzyme pyruvate phosphate dikinase:

$$\text{pyruvate} + \text{Pi} + \text{ATP} \leftrightarrow \text{PEP} + \text{PPi} + \text{AMP}$$

This enzyme is located in the mesophyll chloroplasts, and is activated and inactivated by a very complex mechanism. In the light, it is activated by reducing power from the electron transport chain. In the dark, it is inactivated by a phosphorylation mechanism, in which a phosphate group from ADP is transferred to the enzyme. This phosphorylation requires a second enzyme. Hence, the dikinase will only be active in the light and when ADP rather than ATP is present. Since chloroplast also contain pyruvate kinase, which converts PEP back to pyruvate, this regulation is essential to prevent the oscillation between pyruvate and PEP with the creation of a futile cycle that would waste ATP.

The reaction is reversible but, in the light, the AMP produced in the above reaction is rapidly converted back to ATP by photophosphorylation. It is also thought that the pyrophosphate is rapidly broken down by the enzyme pyrophosphatase to two molecules of inorganic phosphate. Hence, in the light, the reaction would go in the direction of PEP synthesis.

The above scheme describes one form of C_4 mechanism. Other forms are known, but the basic mechanism is the same. In one variant, the transport metabolite between the mesophyll and the bundle sheath is aspartate instead of malate. The decarboxylation reaction in the bundle sheath can also be accomplished by three different enzymes. There are also some plants that appear to be intermediates between true C_3 and C_4 plants.

The mesophyll and bundle sheath tissues are clearly differentiated to perform two quite distinct functions. The chloroplasts in the two tissues are also different, not only in their appearance but also in their biochemistry.

This difference does not result from specialized genomes in the two types of chloroplast, since these are identical. There must, however, be independent expression of the genomes during development. In the C_4 plants in which malate is decarboxylated by the NADP malic enzyme, the chloroplasts lack grana. In these plants NADPH required for photosynthesis is generated solely by the decarboxylation reaction. Hence, photosynthetic NADPH production is not required and grana need not be present. However, ATP is still required and Photosystem I must be active.

The chloroplasts are also differentiated with respect to their enzyme complements. The most striking difference is the lack of RuBPcase in the chloroplasts of the mesophyll and its presence in those from the bundle sheath. Hence, there must not only be control of the nuclear genome for this differentiation but also control of the chloroplast genome in which the large subunit of the carboxylase is encoded. Conversely, the NADP malate dehydrogenase is located only in the chloroplasts of the mesophyll cells.

There is also differential expression of cytosolic enzymes, since phosphoenolpyruvate carboxylase is located exclusively in the mesophyll cells. One strange differentiation of function, so far unexplained, is that sucrose synthesis appears to occur exclusively in the mesophyll cells since sucrose phosphate synthase is found only in these cells. It might have been assumed that sucrose synthesis would have been associated with the bundle sheath cells, since these cells are closely applied to the vascular elements. How the sucrose is transported from the leaf in these plants is not known.

Since C_4 plants have developed a means to overcome the problem of the oxygenase activity of RuBPcase, it might be anticipated that they would be more successful than C_3 plants and hence more abundant. This is not the case. C_4 plants are mainly found in the tropics whereas C_3 plants are dominant in temperate regions. The quantum efficiency, that is number of quanta required to reduce a molecule of carbon dioxide to the carbohydrate level, is similar for both C_3 and C_4 plants at 20°. At higher temperatures, however, the quantum efficiency of C_3 plants is lowered whereas that of C_4 plants is unaffected. Hence, the C_4 plants are more efficient at elevated temperatures. The C_4 plants also continue to show an increase in photosynthesis as the light intensity is increased to full sunlight, whereas C_3 plants saturate much earlier. These differences are a result of different factors limiting photosynthesis under various conditions.

Even though it might be thought that overcoming the oxygenase activity of RuBPcase is the main function of C_4 photosynthesis, a second effect of this metabolism may be more important. The C_4 plants are mainly tropical, and under hot conditions the prevention of the loss of water is of paramount importance. This can only be accomplished by closure of the stomata. However, this prevents effective carbon dioxide uptake. The very high affinity of the C_4 plants for carbon dioxide may allow these plants to close their stomata and still be able to photosynthesize at the reduced levels of carbon dioxide that this causes. Hence, C_4 metabolism may be more related to water stress than oxygen effects. This is carried even further in the CAM plants described in the next chapter.

E

CHAPTER TWELVE

AN ADAPTATION TO XEROPHYTIC CONDITIONS: THE CAM PLANTS

12.1 Introduction

Photosynthesis involves the exchange of carbon dioxide and oxygen which occurs through the stomata of the leaf epidermis. This exchange, however, also means that water is lost from the leaf, which can cause a problem for the plant. Normally, water loss is controlled by the closure of the stomata during water stress. However, for desert plants, opening the stomata during the day—when light is available for photosynthesis—could cause a potentially harmful loss of water. In some plants this problem has been overcome by segregating, on a temporal basis, the fixation and reduction of carbon dioxide. This has some similarities to the situation in C_4 plants, where fixation and reduction are spatially segregated. The enzymes involved in the process are also similar to those described for the C_4 plants. This type of metabolism occurs in succulents, and is usually called crassulacean acid metabolism or CAM metabolism (see Bidwell, 1983; Gardestrom and Edwards, 1985; Osmand and Holtum, 1981; Ting, 1985).

In these plants, the carbon dioxide is fixed at night when the stomata can be opened because the temperature is low and water loss is not so much of a problem. The carbon dioxide is then reduced during the day when light energy is available. Although we normally associate CAM metabolism with plants that live in dry conditions, this form of photosynthesis has been found in other plants; for example, in submerged water plants. In this environment, the carbon dioxide concentration is high at night and low during the day, when the photosynthesis of other plants removes carbon dioxide from the water. In these plants, therefore, CAM metabolism is a strategy to take advantage of the varying concentrations of carbon dioxide.

12.2 The biochemistry of CAM plants

Although more stages are sometimes recognized, there are two distinct phases to CAM photosynthesis. During the night carbon dioxide is fixed and stored and, during the day, it is released and reduced. In the dark, starch reserves in the chloroplast are metabolized, probably via phosphorylase, to triose phosphate. This is transported to the cytosol and is converted to PEP by the enzymes of the glycolytic pathway. Carbon dioxide is fixed by the enzyme phosphoenolpyruvate carboxylase to form oxaloacetate which is then reduced to malate. This malate is the means by which carbon dioxide is stored. The malate is transported to and accumulated in the vacuole. In the dark, large amounts of malate are formed so that the plants can become quite acidic.

In the light, the stomata are closed so that gas exchange with the environment cannot occur and water loss is minimized. Under these conditions, the malate is transported from the vacuole to the chloroplast where it is decarboxylated by the NADP malic enzyme, described earlier, with the release of carbon dioxide for photosynthesis. This is fixed by RuBPcase and then reduced by the reductive pentose phosphate pathway.

The pyruvate released by the decarboxylation is converted back to hexose and stored as starch. The first enzyme of this pathway is pyruvate phosphate dikinase, which was described earlier for the C_4 plants. Once the PEP is formed, the formation of hexose phosphate and starch can occur by the normal gluconeogenic pathway.

The most common CAM plants have the pathway described above. However, as was the case for the C_4 plants, there are variations on this pattern. In all cases, the carbon dioxide is initially fixed as malate. However, the decarboxylation of the malate can be by the three different pathways found in C_4 plants.

CHAPTER THIRTEEN

THE INTERACTION OF THE CHLOROPLAST AND THE CYTOSOL

13.1 Introduction

Chloroplasts have been studied extensively. However, chloroplasts are only one type of plastid, and plastids of some type occur in all parts of a plant, where they perform a variety of functions. In tubers, for example, starch is stored in plastids called amyloplasts. In developing seeds, fatty acid synthesis takes place in colourless plastids called leucoplasts. In all plant tissues, the bulk of the biosynthetic activity of the cell occurs in the plastids. This means that there must be a continual exchange of metabolites between the cytosol and the plastids. However, this exchange must be tightly controlled. This is achieved by the inner membrane of the plastid being impermeable, even to small molecules, so that metabolities must be transported across the membrane by carriers. It is these carriers that control the flux of material into and out of the plastid.

13.2 The phosphate translocator

The importance of the phosphate translocator (see Heber, 1974; Heber and Heldt, 1981) can be judged by the fact that a large percentage of the protein in the inner membrane of the chloroplast is made up of this carrier. It is an exchange carrier which transports inorganic phosphate across the inner membrane in exchange for dihydroxyacetone phosphate or 3-phosphoglycerate. The direction of the transfer depends solely on the concentration of each component on the opposite sides of the membrane.

13.3 The integrated control of starch and sucrose biosynthesis

Starch biosynthesis in chloroplasts (see Preiss *et al.*, 1985; Stitt, 1985; Stitt and Steup, 1985) is an overflow mechanism for storing reduced carbon.

This occurs when the ability of the leaf cell to transport photosynthate cannot keep pace with its production in the chloroplast. On illumination, the initial rate of photosynthesis is low, because the pool of reductive pentose phosphate cycle intermediates is small, and photosynthesis is limited by the supply of ribulose 1,5-bisphosphate. Initially, therefore, the carbon dioxide that is fixed and reduced is used to replenish these pools. Hence, at the start of illumination, there will be a low concentration of dihydroxyacetone phosphate in the chloroplast relative to that of phosphate. Since the phosphate transporter will only exchange dihydroxyacetone for phosphate, under these initial conditions dihydroxyacetone phosphate will not be transported out of the chloroplast.

At a later stage, the concentration of dihydroxyacetone phosphate will increase as the pools of the reductive pentose phosphate pathway are replenished. In contrast, the concentration of inorganic phosphate in the chloroplast will become smaller because phosphate is utilized in photophosphorylation. The ratio of dihydroxyacetone phosphate to inorganic phosphate will, therefore, increase.

At this stage, the concentration of inorganic phosphate in the cytosol will be high relative to that of dihydroxyacetone phosphate. Hence, because of the concentration differences of inorganic phosphate and dihydroxyacetone phosphate across the chloroplast membrane, dihydroxyacetone phosphate in the chloroplast will be exchanged for phosphate from the cytosol. The uptake of this phosphate into the chloroplast is essential if photophosphorylation is to be maintained.

The synthesis of starch is inhibited during the above stages of photosynthesis. Phosphoglycerate is being reduced to dihydroxyacetone phosphate and exported to the cytosol, while inorganic phosphate is being transported into the chloroplast. Hence, the Pi/PGA ratio will be high. Starch biosynthesis is regulated by ADP-glucose pyrophosphorylase. Since this enzyme is inhibited by phosphate and activated by phosphoglycerate, under the initial phases of photosynthesis the enzyme will not be active and starch will not be synthesized.

The dihydroxyacetone phosphate transported to the cytosol will be used for biosynthetic reactions. Any excess will be converted into sucrose and exported from the cell. If the supply of triose phosphate is greater than the ability of the cell to synthesize and export sucrose, then dihydroxyacetone phosphate will build up in the cytosol. This will also result in a decline in the concentration of inorganic phosphate. Under these conditions, the export of dihydroxyacetone from the chloroplast by the phosphate translocator will be inhibited so that dihydroxyacetone will also accumulate in the chloroplast. As the dihydroxyacetone phosphate concentration in the chloroplast increases, the phosphoglycerate concentration will also increase and that of inorganic phosphate decline. The increase in the PGA/Pi ratio will increase the activity of the ADPG-pyrophosphorylase, and starch biosynthesis will be initiated as an overflow store of reduced carbon in the chloroplast.

13.4 The coordination of sucrose synthesis with photosynthetic activity

Sucrose is synthesized in the cytosol of leaf cells from dihydroxyacetone phosphate by a reversal of the glycolytic pathway as far as fructose 1,6-bisphosphate (Stitt, 1985; Stitt and Steup, 1985). Entry of this metabolite into the hexose phosphate pool is catalysed by fructose 1,6-bisphosphatase. It is at this step that sucrose synthesis appears to be regulated. Sucrose phosphate synthase is activated by hexose phosphates, so that as the hexose phosphate pool increases the rate of sucrose synthesis will increase.

The primary indicator of the accumulation of the photosynthetic product dihydroxyacetone phosphate in the cytosol is the metabolic regulator fructose 2,6-bisphosphate. This regulator is not utilized as a cellular metabolite but is an indicator of photosynthetic carbon flux. It is synthesized from fructose 6-phosphate by a specific kinase, fructose 6-phosphate 2-phosphotransferase, which transfers a phosphate group from ATP to the 2-position of fructose 6-phosphate. This enzyme is inhibited by dihydroxyacetone phosphate. Hence, as dihydroxyacetone phosphate accumulates in the cytosol the synthesis of fructose 2,6-bisphosphate stops and the concentration of fructose 2,6-bisphosphate declines.

Fructose 2,6-bisphosphate is a very powerful inhibitor of fructose 1,6-bisphosphatase. As dihydroxyacetone increases in the cytosol and the concentration of fructose 2,6-bisphosphate declines, the inhibition of fructose 1,6-bisphosphatase is relieved and carbon flows into the hexose phosphate pool. The increase in the concentration of the hexose phosphates, in turn, stimulates sucrose phosphate synthase. Hence, sucrose synthesis is integrated with the supply of photosynthate from the chloroplast.

Conversely, when the supply of triose phosphate to the cytosol from the chloroplast is in excess of the ability of the leaf cell to transport sucrose from the leaf so that sucrose accumulates, then sucrose synthesis is inhibited. Under these conditions, the concentration of fructose 2,6-bisphosphate increases; this inhibits fructose 1,6-bisphosphatase and hence the flow of carbon into the hexose phosphate pool. Under these conditions triose phosphate accumulates, and this stimulates starch biosynthesis by the mechanism described above. How the increase in sucrose concentration elevates the level of fructose 2,6-bisphosphate is not known.

Hence the flow of carbon into starch and sucrose is closely integrated. This is achieved by the action of the phosphate translocator in conjunction with the indicator of photosynthate availability, fructose 2,6-bisphosphate.

CHAPTER FOURTEEN

THE COMPARTMENTATION OF PLANT METABOLISM

14.1 Introduction

The importance of compartmentation in plant metabolism (see Dennis and Miernyk, 1982) should have become clear in the previous chapters of this book. Some pathways use a number of compartments, and metabolites are shuttled from one to another during the operation of the pathway. Other pathways, which are entirely cytosolic in animal cells, may be compartmentalized in plants. Many of these pathways occur in the plastids of the plant cell, and the presence of these organelles is one factor that makes plant metabolism different from that of animals.

14.2 The source of plastids and activity of various plastids

Plastids are found in all plant cells, although their mature morphology may be very variable and they may serve a variety of functions (Kirk and Tilney-Bassett, 1978). All plastids are derived from a common proplastid precursor. During tissue differentiation this precursor differentiates into the form of mature plastid that is characteristic of that tissue. The mechanism of this differentiation is unknown. It is probably under nuclear control, since the DNA present in all the plastids of one plant is identical in size and has the same structure.

The enzyme complement of different plastids may be quite different. This is achieved by the import of proteins from the cytosol. These proteins are encoded in the nucleus, translated in the cytosol and then transported into the plastid. The expression of particular nuclear genes for plastid enzymes at various stages of development and in specific tissues will, therefore, determine the metabolic activity of the plastid.

The plastid DNA is not entirely inert in this differentiation (see Dennis *et al.*, 1985). The organellar DNA has enough coding information for at least 120 proteins, although far fewer than this have been identified. It appears that the genes of the plastid DNA can be differentially expressed in different tissues. For example, the chloroplasts of the mesophyll cells of C_4 plants do not contain RuBPcase, whereas those in the bundle sheath cells do contain this enzyme. The DNA of these two types of chloroplast is, however, identical. Since the large subunit of the carboxylase is encoded in the chloroplast DNA, there must be differential regulation of the gene in the two tissues.

The principal site of biosynthetic activity in all plant cells is the plastid (see Dennis and Miernyk, 1982). For example, fatty acids are exclusively formed in this organelle, as are the majority of amino acids and terpenes. In chloroplasts, it probably improves the efficiency of the system to have the site of biosynthetic activity close to the source of ATP and reducing power in the form of NADPH. However, in non-green tissues, where ATP and reducing power have to be imported, most of the biosynthetic activity is still found in the plastid.

Although chloroplasts can be classified as one type of plastid, there are large differences in chloroplast structure in different tissues and at various stages of development. It has clearly been shown that there are large differences in both morphology and metabolism between the mesophyll and bundle sheath chloroplasts of C_4 plants. However, chloroplasts may be different even in other plants that do not show the complex metabolism of C_4 plants. In young leaves that are in an active growth phase, the function of the chloroplasts is to supply metabolites for the growth of the cell. Hence, the enzymic complement of the chloroplasts will reflect this biosynthetic activity. As the leaf matures the main function of the chloroplast will be photosynthesis and, although the organelle will retain some biosynthetic functions, the level of the biosynthetic enzymes will be reduced.

14.3 The function of compartmentation in biosynthetic reactions

The importance of biosynthetic reactions in plant metabolism has been emphasized throughout this book. This constitutes a major difference between plant metabolism and that found in animals. Compartmentation undoubtedly has a role in the control of these various biosynthetic pathways, although much of this control is not yet understood.

The interaction of the various metabolic pools in the organelles of a plant cell is shown in Figure 14.1 (see ap Rees, 1985). In this diagram the

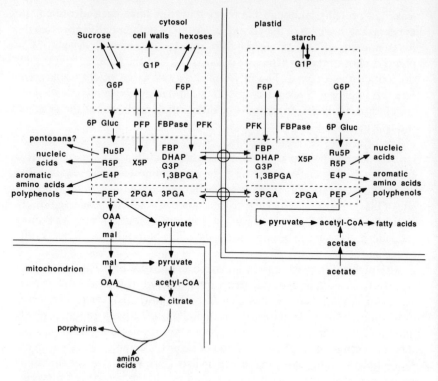

Figure 14.1 A diagramatic representation of the pools of metabolites in a plant cell. Metabolites in equilibrium are enclosed in a dotted line. This does not mean that these metabolites are physically separated. The interaction of the pools in the plastid and the cytosol through the phosphate translocator is also indicated. Based on ap Rees, Stitt, Heldt, Stumpf, Black and Dennis and their co-workers. Abbreviations used are: GIP, glucose 1-phosphate; G6P, glucose 6-phosphate; F6P, fructose 6-phosphate; 6P-GLUC, 6-phosphogluconate; PFP, pyrophosphate dependent phosphofructokinase; FBPase, fructose 1,6-bisphosphatase; PFK, ATP dependent phosphofructokinase; RuBP, ribulose 1,5-bisphosphate; FBP, fructose 1,6-bisphosphate; R5P, ribose 5-phosphate; X5P, xylulose 5-phosphate; DHAP, dihydroxyacetone phosphate; G3P, glyceraldehyde 3-phosphate; E4P, erythrose 4-phosphate, 1,3BPGA, 1,3-bisphosphoglycerate, PEP, phosphoenolpyruvate; 2PGA, 2-phosphglycerate; 3PGA, 3-phosphoglycerate; OAA, oxaloacetate; mal, malate.

reactions between the metabolites that are at equilibrium are not indicated. In the cytosol, there is a hexose phosphate pool. In young tissues, the basic flux of metabolites into this pool will be from sucrose imported from the mature leaves. A large demand on this pool will be for cell wall biosynthesis via the intermediate uridine disphosphate glucose.

The hexose phosphate pool may also provide metabolites for the reversible reactions of the pentose phosphate pathway. Attached to this latter pool in Figure 14.1 are the reactions from glyceraldehyde 3-phosphate to PEP. The flux to PEP will be determined by the ATP/ADP and NAD$^+$/NADH ratios which will be an indication of the energy status of the cell. PEP may be used in mitochondrial metabolism by way of pyruvate or alternatively via malate. The pentose phosphate pool also provides a source of starting materials for various other biosynthetic pathways such as those for nucleic acids, aromatic amino acids and polyphenols. The flux into these compounds may be very great in young cells where not only nucleic acids are required but also aromatic amino acids for proteins and lignins. Also shown in the diagram is a pathway into pentosans which are other components of cell walls. However, it is generally assumed that pentosans are synthesized from UDPG, although a direct incorporation from pentoses has not been excluded at this time.

A principal function of the tricarboxylic acid cycle of the mitochondrion is the formation of ATP. However, it must be remembered that it is also a source of metabolic intermediates for the synthesis of amino acids and porphyrins. In young tissue, this may be a major function of this organelle. In older leaf tissue, the mitochondrion will also have a major role in photorespiration.

The flux of metabolites from the hexose phosphate pool into the reversible reactions of the pentose phosphate pathway is via three routes. The first route is via the oxidative reactions of the pentose phosphate pathway which will be active when the NADPH/NADP$^+$ ratio is low. Under these conditions, the pentose phosphate pathway may act as a cycle but it can also act as a source of trioses for the glycolytic pathway. The second route is via the ATP-dependent phosphofructokinase. This enzyme is powerfully inhibited by PEP, and hence will be active only when this compound is being utilized by mitochondrial metabolism. This enzyme is also activated by inorganic phosphate, an indicator of active mitochondrial metabolism.

The third route of flux from the hexose phosphate pool into the reversible pentose phosphate pathway is via the pyrophosphate-dependent phosphofructokinase (Black et al., 1985). Unlike the ATP-dependent phosphofructokinase, this enzyme is not regulated by glycolytic intermediates but by fructose 2,6-bisphosphate which is a powerful activator of the enzyme. Fructose 2,6-bisphosphate is an indicator of active metabolic tissues. The pyrophosphate-dependent phosphofructokinase, unlike the ATP-dependent enzyme, is reversible and it may serve to equilibrate the hexose phosphate and pentose phosphate pools at times of high biosynthetic activity. At such times there will be a large supply of pyrophosphate which is a byproduct of polysaccharide biosynthesis.

The reversible reactions of the pentose phosphate pathway in the cytosol will equilibrate with a similar pool in the plastid through the phosphate translocator. The direction of flow of metabolites will depend on the concentration of dihydroxyacetone phosphate, 3-phosphoglycerate and inorganic phosphate on each side of the plastid membrane. Also in the plastid is a hexose phosphate pool. This pool is used for starch biosynthesis. The rate of starch synthesis is controlled by the PGA/Pi ratio since ADPG pyrophosphorylase is activated by 3-phosphoglycerate and inhibited by Pi (Preiss *et al.*, 1985; Stitt and Steup, 1985). In contrast, starch phosphorylase requires high concentrations of Pi.

Plastids do not contain the pyrophosphate-dependent phosphofructokinase. However, they do contain the oxidative reactions of the pentose phosphate pathway and the ATP-dependent phosphofructokinase. These are basically under the same control as their cytosolic counterparts. The lack of the pyrophosphate phosphofructokinase may reflect the fact that plastid hexose phosphate pool is only used for starch biosynthesis and no other synthetic reactions, unlike its cytosolic counterpart.

The flux of metabolites from the pentose phosphate pathway into the hexose phosphate pool is catalysed by fructose 1,6-bisphosphatase. In green tissues, this enzyme is activated by light, which is an indicator of active photosynthesis and hence of a flux of carbon into the pentose phosphate pathway. In this respect, it must be remembered that, in green leaves, the oxidative and reductive pentose phosphate pathways will both be present.

The formation of phosphoenolpyruvate from 3-phosphoglyceric acid may not occur in mature chloroplasts, although it does occur in some plastids. The plastid phosphofructokinase is powerfully inhibited by phosphoenolpyruvate and also by 3-phosphoglycerate. It is activated by inorganic phosphate. Hence, the flux from the hexose phosphate pool will be controlled by the utilization of metabolites in the pentose phosphate pathway. In metabolically active tissues, PEP will be used for pyruvate formation which is an intermediate in fatty acid biosynthesis. In Figure 14.1 aromatic amino acid biosynthesis is shown as occurring in both the cytosol and the plastid. The enzymes of the pathway have been shown to be present in plastids although some enzymes of this pathway have also been found in the cytosol.

The interconversion of sucrose and starch is important in plant cells

(Stitt and Steup, 1985). This is especially the case in leaves. The regulation of this interconversion by fructose 2,6-phosphate through its action on the cytosolic fructose 1,6-bisphosphatase has already been described. The segregation of starch and sucrose biosynthesis into these two compartments may be the only means by which their interconversion can be controlled.

It is clear that plant metabolism is complex, and much more research is required before it is fully understood. In particular, the regulation of the pathways in the various cell compartments needs to be explored as does the control of the transport of metabolites across the membranes of the organelles.

In 1961, Harry Beevers published his classic book on plant respiration (Beevers, 1961). Much progress has been made since then, and it can be anticipated that as much, if not more, will be achieved in the next twenty-five years.

REFERENCES AND FURTHER READING

Chapters 1 and 2

Atkinson, D.E. (1977) *Cellular Energy Metabolism and Its Regulation*. Academic Press Inc.

Forti, G. (1977) 'Flavoproteins', in *Encyclopedia of Plant Physiology, New Series* (A. Pirson and M.H. Zimmermann, eds.), Vol. 5, *Photosynthesis I. Photosynthetic Electron Transport and Photophosphorylation* (A. Trebst and M. Avron, eds.), Springer Verlag, Berlin, 222–226.

Goodwin, T.W. and Mercer, E.I. (1983) *Introduction to Plant Biochemistry*, 2nd edition. Pergamon Press, Oxford.

Lehninger, A.L. (1971) *Bioenergetics: The Molecular Basis of Biological Energy Transformations*. W.A. Benjamin, California.

Morowitz, H.J. (1978) *Foundations of Bioenergetics*. Academic Press, New York.

Morris, J.G. (1974) *A Biologist's Physical Chemistry*, 2nd edition. Edward Arnold, London.

Palmer, G. (1975) 'Iron-sulfur proteins', in *The Enzymes* (P.D. Boyer, ed.), Vol. XII, Academic Press, New York, 2–56.

Pradet, A. and Raymond, P. (1983) Adenine nucleotide ratios and adenylate energy charge in energy metabolism. *Ann. Rev. Pl. Physiol.* **34**, 199–224.

Smith, E.L., Hill, R.L.,Lehman, I.R., Lefkowitz, R.J., Handler, P. and White, A. (1983) *Principles of Biochemistry: General Aspects*, 7th edition, McGraw-Hill, New York, 241–258.

Stryer, L. (1981) *Biochemistry*, 2nd edition. W.H. Freeman and Co., San Francisco, 235–247.

Chapter 3

Chance, B. (1977) Electron transfer: pathways, mechanisms and controls, *Ann. Rev. Biochem.* **46**, 967–980.

Dennis, D.T. (1983) 'Energy metabolism in plants', in *Plant Physiology: A Treatise* (F.C. Steward, ed), Vol. VII, *Energy and Carbon Metabolism* (F.C. Steward and R.G.S. Bidwell, eds.), Academic Press, New York, 163–286.

Ernster, L. (1977) Chemical and chemiosmotic aspects of electron transport-linked phosphorylation. *Ann. Rev. Biochem.* **46**, 981–995.

Mitchell, P. (1961) Coupling of phosphorylation to electron and hydrogen transfer by a chemiosmotic type of mechanism. *Nature (London)* **191**, 144–148.

Mitchell, P. (1966) Chemiosmotic coupling in oxidative and photosynthetic phosphorylation. *Biol. Rev.* **41**, 445–502.

Mitchell, P. (1972) Structural and functional organization of energy-transducing membranes and their ion-conducting properties. *FEBS Symp.* **28**, 353–370.

Mitchell, P. (1976) Vectorial chemistry and the molecular mechanics of chemiosmotic coupling: power transmission by proticity, *Biochem. Soc. Trans.* **4**, 399–430.

Mitchell, P. (1977) Vectorial chemiosmotic processes. *Ann. Rev. Biochem.* **46**, 996–1005.

Nicholls, D.G. (1982) *Bioenergetics: An Introduction to the Chemiosmotic Theory.* Academic Press, London.

Williams, R.J.P. (1978) The multifarious couplings of energy transduction. *Biochim. Biophys. Acta* **505**, 1–44.

Chapter 4

Baird, B.A. and Hammes, G.G. (1979) Structure of oxidative- and photo-phosphorylation coupling factor complexes. *Biochim. Biophys. Acta* **549**, 31–53.

Boyer, P.D. (1977) Coupling mechanisms in capture, transmission and use of energy. *Ann. Rev. Biochem.* **46**, 957–966.

Boyer, P.D. (1977) Conformational coupling in oxidative phosphorylation and photophosphorylation. *Trends in Biochem. Sci.* **2**, 38–41.

Cross, R.L. (1981) The mechanism and regulation of ATP synthesis by F_1-ATPases. *Ann. Rev. Biochem.* **50**, 681–714.

Day, D.A., Arron, G.P. and Laties, G.C. (1980) 'Nature and control of respiratory pathways in plants: the interaction of cyanide-resistant respiration with the cyanide-sensitive pathway', in *The Biochemistry of Plants* (E.E. Conn and P.K. Stumpf, eds.), Vol. 2, Academic Press, New York, 197–241.

Dennis, D.T. (1983) 'Energy metabolism in plants', in *Plant Physiology: A Treatise* (F.C. Steward, ed.), Vol. VII, *Energy and Carbon Metabolism* (F.C. Steward and R.G.S. Bidwell, eds), Academic Press, New York, 163–286.

Douce, R. (1985) *Mitochondria in Higher Plants: Structure, Function, and Biogenesis.* American Society of Plant Physiologists Monograph Series, Academic Press, New York.

Ducet, G. (1985) Plant Mitochondrial Cytochromes. In: *Encyclopedia of Plant Physiology, New Series*, Vol. 18. *Higher Plant Cell Respiration* (R. Douce and D.A. Day, eds.), Springer Verlag, Berlin, 72–105.

Fillingame, R.H. (1980) The proton-translocating pumps of oxidative phosphorylation. *Ann. Rev. Biochem.* **49**, 1079–1113.

Hatefi, Y. (1985) The mitochondrial electron transport and oxidative phosphorylation system. *Ann. Rev. Biochem.* **54**, 1015–1020.

Lambers, H. (1985) 'Respiration in intact plants and tissues: its regulation and dependence on environmental factors, metabolism and invading organisms', in *Encyclopedia of Plant Physiology, New Series*, Vol. 18, *Higher Plant Cell Respiration* (R. Douce and D.A. Day, eds.), Springer Verlag, Berlin, 418–474.

Lance, C., Chauvean, M. and Dizengremel, P. (1985) 'The cyanide-resistant pathway of plant mitochondria', in *Encyclopedia of Plant Physiology, New Series*, Vol. 18, *Higher Plant Cell Respiration* (R. Douce and D.A. Day, eds.), Springer Verlag, Berlin, 202–247.

Laties, G.G. (1982) The cyanide-resistant, alternative path in higher plant respiration. *Ann. Rev. Pl. Physiol.* **33**, 519–555.

Meeuse, B.J.D. (1975) Thermogenic respiration in aroids. *Ann. Rev. Pl. Physiol.* **26**, 117–126.

Mitchell, P. (1961) Coupling of phosphorylation to electron and hydrogen transfer by a chemiosmotic type of mechanism, *Nature (London)* **191**, 144–148.

Mitchell, P. (1966) Chemiosmotic coupling in oxidative and photosynthetic phosphorylation. *Biol. Rev.*, **41**, 445–502.

Moore, A.L. and Rich, P.R. (1980) The bioenergetics of plant mitochondria. *Trends in Biochem. Sci.* **5**, 284–288.

Moore, A.L. and Rich, P.R. (1985) 'Organization of the respiratory chain and oxidative phosphorylation', in *Encyclopedia of Plant Physiology, New Series*, Vol. 18, *Higher Plant Cell Respiration* (R. Douce and D.A. Day, eds.), Springer Verlag, Berlin, 134–172.

Nicholls, D.G. (1982) *Bioenergetics: An Introduction to the Chemiosmotic Theory.* Academic Press, London.

Papa, S. (1976) Proton translocation reactions in the respiratory chains. *Biochim. Biophys. Acta* **456**, 39—84.

Palmer, J.M. and Ward, J.A. (1985) 'The oxidation of NADH by plant mitochondria', in *Encyclopedia of Plant Physiology, New Series*, Vol. 18, *Higher Plant Cell Respiration* (R. Douce and D.A. Day, eds.), Springer Verlag, Berlin, 173–201.

Racker, E. (1977) Mechanisms of energy transformations. *Ann. Rev. Biochem.* **46**, 1006–1014.

Rieske, J.S. (1976) Composition, structure and function of complex III of the respiratory chain. *Biochim. Biophys. Acta* **456**, 195–247.

Solomos, T. (1977) Cyanide-resistant respiration in higher plants. *Ann. Rev. Pl. Physiol.* **28**, 279–297.

Storey, B.T. (1980) 'Electron transport and energy coupling in plant mitochondria', in *The Biochemistry of Plants* (E.E. Conn and P.K. Stumpf, eds.), Vol. 2, Academic Press, New York, 125–195.

Wilkstrom, M., Krab, K. and Saraste, M. (1981) Proton-translocating cytochrome complexes. *Ann. Rev. Biochem.* **50**, 623–656.

Chapter 5

Amesz, J. (1977) 'Plastoquinone', in *Encyclopedia of Plant Physiology, New Series* (A. Pirson and M.H. Zimmermann, eds.), Vol. 5, *Photosynthesis I. Photosynthetic Electron Transport and Phosphorylation* (A. Trebst and M. Avron, eds.), Springer Verlag, Berlin, 238–246.

Arnon, D.I. (1977) 'Photosynthesis 1950–75: changing concepts and perspectives', in *Encyclopedia of Plant Physiology, New Series* (A. Pirson and M.H. Zimmerman, eds.), Vol. 5, *Photosynthesis I. Photosynthetic Electron Transport and Photophosphorylation* (A. Trebst and M. Avron, eds.), Springer Verlag, Berlin, 7–56.

Arntzen, C.J. (1978) Dynamic structural features of chloroplast lamellae. *Curr. Top. Bioenerg.* **8**, 111–160.

Avron, M. (1981) 'Photosynthetic Electron Transport and Photophosphorylation', in *The Biochemistry of Plants: A Comprehensive Treatise* (P.K. Stumpf and E.E. Conn, eds.), Vol. 8, *Photosynthesis* (M.D. Hatch and N.K. Boardman, eds.), Academic Press, New York, 164–193.

Baird, B.A. and Hammes, G.G. (1979) Structure of oxidative- and photo-phosphorylation coupling factor complexes. *Biochim. Biophys. Acta* **549**, 31–53.

Cogdell, R.J. (1983) Photosynthetic reaction centres. *Ann. Rev. Pl. Physiol.* **34**, 21–45.

Cramer, W.A. and Whitmarsh, J. (1977) Photosynthetic cytochromes, *Ann. Rev. Pl. Physiol.* **28**, 133–172.

Dennis, D.T. (1983) 'Energy metabolism in plants', in *Plant Physiology: A Treatise* (F.C. Steward ed), Vol. VII, *Energy and Carbon Metabolism* (F.C. Steward and R.G.S. Bidwell eds.), Academic Press, New York, 163–286.

Diner, B.A. and Joliot, P. (1977) 'Oxygen Evolution and Manganese', in *Encyclopedia of Plant Physiology, New Series* (A. Pirson and M.H. Zimmermann, eds.), Vol. 5, *Photosynthesis I. Photosynthetic Electron Transport and Photophosphorylation* (A. Trebst and M. Avron, eds.), Springer Verlag, Berlin, 187–205.

Gimmler, H. (1977) 'Photophosphorylation *in vivo*', in *Encyclopedia of Plant Physiology, New Series* (A. Pirson and M.H. Zimmerman, eds.), Vol. 5, *Photosynthesis I. Photosynthetic Electron Transport and Photophosphorylation* (A. Trebst and M. Avron, eds.), Springer Verlag, Berlin, 448–472.

Goldbeck, J.H., Lien, S. and San Pietro, A. (1977) 'Electron Transport in Chloroplasts', in *Encyclopedia of Plant Physiology* (A. Pirson and M.H. Zimmermann, eds.), Vol. 5,

Photosynthetic Electron Transport and Photophosphorylation (A. Trebst and M. Avron, eds.), Springer Verlag, Berlin, 94–116.

Gregory, R.P.F. (1978) *Biochemistry of Photosynthesis*, 2nd edition. Wiley, Chichester.

Haehnel, W. (1984) Photosynthetic electron transport in higher plants. *Ann. Rev. Pl. Physiol.* **35**, 659–693.

Hall, D.O. and Rao, K.K. (1977) 'Ferredoxin', in *Encyclopedia of Plant Physiology, New Series* (A. Pirson and M.H. Zimmermann, eds.), Vol. 5, *Photosynthetic Electron Transport and Photophosphorylation* (A. Trebst and M. Avron, eds.), Springer Verlag, Berlin, 206–216.

Hauska, G. and Trebst, A. (1977) Proton translocation in chloroplasts. *Current Topics Bioenerg.* **6**, 151–220.

Jagendorf, A.T. (1977) 'Photophosphorylation', in *Encyclopedia of Plant Physiology, New Series* (A. Pirson and M.H. Zimmermann, eds.), Vol. 5, *Photosynthesis I. Photosynthetic Electron Transport and Photophosphorylation* (A. Trebst and M. Avron, eds.), Springer Verlag, Berlin, 307–337.

Junge, W. (1977) 'Physical aspects of light harvesting electron transport and electrochemical potential generation in photosynthesis of green plants', in *Encyclopedia of Plant Physiology, New Series* (A. Pirson and M.H. Zimmermann, eds.), Vol. 5, *Photosynthesis I. Photosynthetic Electron Transport and Photophosphorylation* (A. Trebst and M. Avron, eds.), Springer Verlag, Berlin, 59–93.

Katoh, S. (1977) 'Plastocyanin', in *Encyclopedia of Plant Physiology, New Series* (A. Pirson and M.H. Zimmermann, eds.), Vol. 5, *Photosynthesis I. Photosynthetic Electron Transport and Photophosphorylation* (A. Trebst and M. Avron, eds.), Springer Verlag, Berlin, 247–252.

Ke, B. (1978) The primary electron acceptors in green-plant photosystem I and photosynthetic bacteria. *Current Topics Bioenerg.* **7**, 75–138.

Malkin, R. (1982) Photosystem I. *Ann. Rev. Pl. Physiol.* **33**, 455–479.

Malkin, R. and Bearden, A.J. (1978) Membrane-bound iron-sulfur centers in photosynthetic systems. *Biochim. Biophys. Acta* **505**, 147–181.

Mathis, P. and Paillotin, G. (1981) 'Primary processes of photosynthesis', in *The Biochemistry of Plants: A Comprehensive Treatise* (P.K. Stumpf and E.E. Conn, eds.), Vol. 8, *Photosynthesis* (M.D. Hatch and N.K. Boardman, eds.), Academic Press, New York, 98–163.

Sane, P.V. (1977) 'The topography of the thylakoid membrane of the chloroplast', in *Encyclopedia of Plant Physiology, New Series* (A. Pirson and M.H. Zimmermann, eds.), Vol. 5, *Photosynthesis I. Photosynthetic Electron Transport and Photophosphorylation* (A. Trebst and M. Avron, eds.), Springer Verlag, Berlin, 522–542.

Shavit, N. (1980) Energy transduction in chloroplasts: structure and function of the ATPase complex. *Ann. Rev. Biochem.* **49**, 111–138.

Strotmann, H. and Bickel-Sandkotter, S. (1984) Structure, function and regulation of chloroplast ATPase. *Ann. Rev. Pl. Physiol.* **35**, 97–120.

Velthuys, B.R. (1980) Mechanisms of electron flow in photosystem II toward photosystem I. *Ann. Rev. Pl. Physiol.* **31**, 545–567.

Chapter 6

Akazawa, T. and Okamoto, K. (1980) 'Biosynthesis and metabolism of sucrose', in *The Biochemistry of Plants: A Comprehensive Treatise* (P.K. Stumpf and E.E. Conn, eds.), Vol. 3, *Carbohydrates: Structure and Function* (J. Preiss, ed.), Academic Press, New York, 199–220.

ap Rees, T. (1980) 'Integration of pathways of synthesis and degradation of hexose phosphates', in *The Biochemistry of Plants* (P.K. Stumpf and E.E. Conn, eds.), Vol. 3. *Carbohydrates: Structure and Function* (J. Preiss, ed.), Academic Press, New York, 1–42.

ap Rees, T. (1985) 'The organization of glycolysis and the oxidative pentose phosphate pathway in plants', in *Encyclopedia of Plant Physiology, New Series*, Vol. 18, *Higher Plant Cell Respiration* (R. Douce and D.A. Day, eds.), Springer Verlag, Berlin, 391–417.

Davies, D.D. (1979) The central role of phosphoenolpyruvate in plant metabolism. *Ann. Rev. Pl. Physiol.* **30**, 131–158.

Ericson, M.C. and Elbein, A.D. (1980) 'Biosynthesis of cell wall polysaccharides and glycoproteins', in *The Biochemistry of Plants: A Comprehensive Treatise* (P.K. Stumpf and E.E. Conn, eds.), Vol. 3. *Carbohydrates: Structure and Function* (J. Preiss, ed.), Academic Press, New York, 589–616.

Feingold, D.S. and Avigad, G. (1980) 'Sugar nucleotide transformations in plants', in *The Biochemistry of Plants: A Comprehensive Treatise* (P.K. Stumpf and E.E. Conn, eds.), Vol. 3, *Carbohydrates: Structure and Function* (J. Preiss, ed.), Academic Press, New York, 102–170.

Preiss, J. (1982) Regulation of the biosynthesis and degradation of starch. *Ann. Rev. Pl. Physiol.* **33**, 431–454.

Preiss, J. and Levi, C. (1980) 'Starch biosynthesis and degradation', in *The Biochemistry of Plants: A Comprehensive Treatise* (P.K. Stumpf and E.E. Conn, eds.), Vol. 3, *Carbohydrates: Structure and Function* (J. Preiss, ed.), Academic Press, New York, 371–424.

Stitt, M. and Steup, M. (1985) 'Starch and sucrose degradation', in *Encyclopedia of Plant Physiology, New Series*, Vol. 18, *Higher Plant Cell Respiration* (R. Douce and D.A. Day, eds.), Springer Verlag, Berlin, 347–390.

Chapter 7

Davies, D.D. (1979) The central role of phosphenolpyruvate in plant metabolism. *Ann. Rev. Pl. Physiol.* **30**, 131–158.

Douce, R. (1985) *Mitochondria in Higher Plants: Structure, Function, and Biogenesis*, American Society of Plant Physiologists Monograph Series, Academic Press, New York.

Hanson, J.B. (1985) 'Membrane transport systems of plant mitochondria', in *Encyclopedia of Plant Physiology, New Series*, Vol. 18, *Higher Plant Cell Respiration* (R. Douce and D.A. Day, eds.), Springer Verlag, Berlin, 248–280.

Wiskich, J.T. and Dry, I.B. (1985) 'The tricarboxylic acid cycle in plant mitochondria: its operation and regulation', in *Encyclopedia of Plant Physiology, New Series*, Vol. 18, *Higher Plant Cell Respiration* (R. Douce and D.A. Day, eds.), Springer Verlag, Berlin, 281–313.

Chapter 8

Alberts, A.W. and Greenspan, M.D. (1984) 'Animal and bacterial fatty acid synthetase: structure, function and regulation', in *Fatty Acid Metabolism and Its Regulation* (S. Numa, ed.), *New Comprehensive Biochemistry*, Vol. 7 (A. Neuberger and L.L.M van Deenen, eds.), Elsevier, Amsterdam, 29–58.

Beevers, H. (1978) 'The role of mitochondria in fatty seedling tissues', in *Plant Mitochondria* (G. Ducet and C. Lance, eds.), Elsevier/North-Holland, Amsterdam, 365–72.

Beevers, H. (1979) Microbodies in higher plants. *Ann. Rev. Pl. Physiol.* **30**, 159–193.

Beevers, H. (1980) 'The role of the glyoxylate cycle', in *The Biochemistry of Plants* (P.K. Stumpf and E.E. Conn, eds.), Vol. 4, *Lipids: Structure and Function* (P.K. Stumpf, ed.), Academic Press, New York, 117–131.

Bremer, J. and Osmundsen, H. (1984) 'Fatty acid oxidation and its regulation', in *Fatty Acid*

Metabolism and Its Regulation (S. Numa, ed.), *New Comprehensive Biochemistry*, Vol. 7. (A. Neuberger and L.L.M. van Deenen, eds.), Elsevier, Amsterdam, 113–154.

Dennis, D.T. and Miernyk, J.A. (1982) Compartmentation of nonphotosynthetic carbohydrate metabolism. *Ann. Rev. Plant Physiol.* **33**, 27–50.

Kindl, H. (1984) 'Lipid degradation in higher plants', in *Fatty Acid Metabolism and Its Regulation* (S. Numa, ed.), *New Comprehensive Biochemistry*, Vol. 7 (A. Neuberger and L.L.M. van Deenen, eds.), Elsevier, Amsterdam, 181–204.

Mettler, I.J. and Beevers, H. (1980) Oxidation of NADH in glyoxysomes by a malate-aspartate shuttle. *Pl. Physiol.* **66**, 555–560.

Numa, S. and Tanabe, T. (1984) 'Acetyl-coenzyme A carboxylase and its regulation', in *Fatty Acid Metabolism and Its Regulation* (S. Numa, ed.), *New Comprehensive Biochemistry*, Vol. 7 (A. Neuberger and L.L.M. van Deenen, eds.), Elsevier, Amsterdam, 1–28.

Ohlrogge, J.B., Kuhn, D.N., Stumpf, P.K. (1979) Subcellular localization of acyl carrier protein in leaf protoplasts of *Spinacia oleraceae*. *Proc. Natl. Acad. Sci. USA* **76**, 1194–1198.

Stumpf, P.K. (1980) 'Biosynthesis of saturated and unsaturated fatty acids', in *The Biochemistry of Plants* (P.K. Stumpf and E.E. Conn, eds.), Vol. 4, *Lipids: Structure and Function* (P.K. Stumpf, ed.), Academic Press, New York, 177–204.

Stumpf, P.K. (1984) 'Fatty acid biosynthesis in higher plants', in *Fatty Acid Metabolism and Its Regulation* (S. Numa, ed.), *New Comprehensive Biochemistry*, Vol. 7 (A. Neuberger and L.L.M. van Deenen, eds.), Elsevier, Amsterdam, 155–180.

Tolbert, N.E. (1981) Metabolic pathways in peroxisomes and glyoxysomes. *Ann. Rev. Biochem.* **50**, 133–158.

Trelease, R.N. (1984) Biogenesis of glyoxysomes. *Ann. Rev. Pl. Physiol.* **35**, 321–347.

Trelease, R.N. and Doman, D.C. (1984) 'Mobilization of oil and wax reserves', in *Seed Physiology*, Vol. 2 (D.L. Murray, ed.), Academic Press, Australia, 201–245.

Wakil, S.J., Stoops, J.K. and Joshi, V.C. (1983) Fatty acid synthesis and its regulation. *Ann. Rev. Biochem.* **52**, 537–580.

Chapter 9

Bidwell, R.G.S. (1983) 'Carbon nutrition of plants: photosynthesis and respiration', in *Plant Physiology: A Treatise* (F.C. Steward, ed.), Vol. VII. *Energy and Carbon Metabolism* (F.C. Steward and R.G.S. Bidwell, eds.), Academic Press, New York, 287–458.

Buchanan, B.B. (1980) Role of light in the regulation of chloroplast enzymes. *Ann. Rev. Plant Physiol.* **31**, 341–374.

Buchanan, B.B., Wolosiuk, R.A. and Schurmann, P. (1979) Thioredoxin and enzyme regulation. *Trends Biochem. Sci.* **4**, 93–96.

Gregory, R.P.F. (1978) *Biochemistry of Photosynthesis*, 2nd edition. Wiley, Chichester.

Lorimer, G.H. (1981) The carboxylation and oxygenation of ribulose 1,5-bisphosphate: the primary events in photosynthesis and photorespiration. *Ann. Rev. Pl. Physiol.* **32**, 349–384.

Lorimer, G.H. and Andrews, T.J. (1981) 'The C_2 chemo- and photorespiratory carbon oxidation cycle', in *The Biochemistry of Plants: A Comprehensive Treatise* (P.K. Stumpf and E.E. Conn, eds.) Vol. 8, *Photosynthesis* (M.D. Hatch and N.K. Boardman, eds.), Academic Press, New York, 330–375.

Miziorko, H.M. and Lorimer, G.H. (1983) Ribulose 1,5-bisphosphate carboxylase-oxygenase. *Ann. Rev. Biochem.* **52**, 507–536.

Robinson, S.P. and Walker, D.A. (1981) 'Photosynthetic carbon reduction cycle', in *The Biochemistry of Plants: A Comprehensive Treatise* (P.K. Stumpf and E.E. Conn, eds.), Vol. 8, *Photosynthesis* (M.D. Hatch and N.K. Boardman, eds.), Academic Press, New York, 194–237.

Chapter 10

Beevers, H. (1979) Microbodies in higher plants. *Ann. Rev. Pl. Physiol.* **30**, 159–93.

Bidwell, R.G.S. (1983) 'Carbon nutrition of plants: photosynthesis and respiration', in *Plant Physiology: A Treatise* (F.C. Steward, ed.), Vol. VII, *Energy and Carbon Metabolism* (F.C. Steward and R.G.S. Bidwell, eds.), Academic Press, New York, 287–458.

Douce, R. (1985) 'The mechanism of glycine oxidation', in *Mitochondria in Higher Plants: Structure, Functions, Biogenesis* (R. Douce, ed.), Academic Press, New York, 190–203.

Lorimer, G.H. (1981) 'The carboxylation and oxygenation of ribulose 1,5-bisphosphate: the primary events in photosynthesis and photorespiration. *Ann. Rev. Pl. Physiol.* **32**, 349–384.

Lorimer, G.H. and Andrews, T.J. (1981) 'The C_2 chemo- and photorespiratory carbon oxidation cycle', in *The Biochemistry of Plants: A Comprehensive Treatise* (P.K. Stumpf and E.E. Conn. eds.), Vol. 8, *Photosynthesis* (M.D. Hatch and N.K. Boardman, eds.), Academic Press, New York, 330–375.

Miziorko, H.M. and Lorimer, G.H. (1983) Ribulose 1,5-bisphosphate carboxylase-oxygenase. *Ann. Rev. Biochem.* **52**, 507–536.

Tolbert, N.E. (1981) Metabolic pathways in peroxisomes and glyoxysomes. *Ann. Rev. Biochem.* **50**, 133–158.

Chapter 11

Bidwell, R.G.S. (1983) 'Carbon nutrition of plants: photosynthesis and respiration', in *Plant Physiology: A Treatise* (F.C. Steward, ed.), Vol. VII, *Energy and Carbon Metabolism* (F.C. Steward and R.G.S. Bidwell, eds.), Academic Press, New York, 287–458.

Edwards, G.E. and Huber, S.C. (1981) 'The C_4 pathway', in *The Biochemistry of Plants: A Comprehensive Treatise* (P.K. Stumpf and E.E. Conn, eds.), Vol. 8, *Photosynthesis* (M.D. Hatch and N.K. Boardman, eds.), Academic Press, New York, 238–282.

Edwards, G.E., Nakamoto, H., Burnell, J.N. and Hatch, M.D. (1985) Pyruvate, Pi dikinase and NADP-malate dehydrogenase in C_4 photosynthesis: properties and mechanism of light/dark regulation. *Ann. Rev. Pl. Physiol.* **36**, 255–286.

Gardestrom, P. and Edwards, G.E. (1985) 'Leaf mitochondria $(C_3 + C_4 + CAM)$', in *Encyclopedia of Plant Physiology, New Series.* Vol. 18, *Higher Plant Cell Respiration* (R. Douce and D.A. Day, eds.), Springer Verlag, Berlin, 314–346.

Ogren, W.L. (1984) Photorespiration: pathways, regulation modification. *Ann. Rev. Pl. Physiol.* **35**, 415–442.

Chapter 12

Bidwell, R.G.S. (1983) 'Carbon nutrition of plants: photosynthesis and respiration', in *Plant Physiology: A Treatise* (F.C. Steward, ed.), Vol. VII. *Energy and Carbon Metabolism* (F.C. Steward and R.G.S. Bidwell, eds.), Academic Press, New York, 287–458.

Gardestrom, P. and Edwards, G.E. (1985) 'Leaf mitochondria $(C_3 + C_4 + CAM)$', in *Encyclopedia of Plant Physiology, New Series*, Vol. 18, *Higher Plant Cell Respiration* (R. Douce and D.A. Day, eds.), Springer Verlag, Berlin, 314–346.

Osmond, G.B. and Holtum, J.A.M. (1981) 'Crassulacean acid metabolism,' in *The Biochemistry of Plants: A Comprehensive Treatise* (P.K. Stumpf and E.E. Conn, eds), Vol. 8, *Photosynthesis*, (M.D. Hatch and N.K. Boardman, eds.), Academic Press, New York, 283–329.

Ting, I.P. (1985) Crassulacean acid metabolism. *Ann. Rev. Pl. Physiol.* **36**, 595–622.

Chapter 13

Heber, U. (1974) Metabolite exchange between chloroplasts and cytoplasm. *Ann. Rev. Pl. Physiol.* **25**, 393–421.

Heber, U. and Heldt, H.W. (1981) The chloroplast envelope: Structure, function and role in leaf metabolism. *Ann. Rev. Pl. Physiol.* **32**, 139–168.

Preiss, J., Robinson, N., Spilatro, S. and McNamara, K. (1985) 'Starch synthesis and its regulation,' in *Regulation of Carbon Partitioning in Photosynthetic Tissue* (R.L. Heath and J. Preiss, eds.), Proc. Eighth Ann. Symp. Pl. Physiol., University of Riverside. Amer. Soc. Plant Physiol., Waverly Press, Maryland.

Stitt, M. (1985) 'Fine control of sucrose synthesis by fructose 2;6-bisphosphate', in *Regulation of Carbon Partitioning in Photosynthetic Tissue* (R.L. Heath and J. Preiss, eds.), Proc. Eighth Ann. Symp. Pl. Physiol., University of Riverside. Amer. Soc. Plant Physiol., Waverly Press, Maryland.

Stitt, M. and Steup, M. (1985) (Starch and sucrose degradation,' in *Encyclopedia of Plant Physiology, New Series*, Vol. 18, *Higher Plant Cell Respiration* (R. Douce and D.A. Day, eds.), Springer Verlag, Berlin, 347–390.

Chapter 14

Beevers, H. (1961) *Respiratory Metabolism in Plants.* Harpers, New York.

ap Rees, T. (1985) 'The organization of glycolysis and the oxidative pentose phosphate pathway in plants,' in *Encyclopedia of Plant Physiology*, New Series, Vol. 18, *Higher Plant Cell Respiration* (R. Douce and D.A. Day, eds.), Springer Verlag, Berlin, 391–417.

Black, C.C., Carnal, N.W. and Paz, N. (1985) Roles of pyrophosphate and fructose 2;6-bisphosphate in regulating plant sugar metabolism,' in *Regulation of Carbon Partitioning in Photosynthetic Tissue* (R.L. Heath and J. Preiss, eds.) Proc. Eighth Ann. Symp. Pl. Physiol., University of Riverside. Amer. Soc. Pl. Physiol., Waverly Press, Maryland.

Dennis, D.T., Hekman, W.E., Thomson, A., Ireland, R.J., Botha, F.C. and Kruger, N.J. (1985) 'Compartmentation of Glycolytic Enzymes in Plants,' in *Regulation of Carbon Partitioning in Photosynthetic Tissue* (R.L. Heath and J. Preiss, eds.) Proc. Eighth Ann. Symp. Pl. Physiol., University of Riverside. Amer. Soc. Plant Physiol., Waverly Press, Maryland.

Dennis, D.T. and Miernyk, J.A. (1982) 'Compartmentation of Nonphotosynthetic Carbohydrate Metabolism', *Ann. Rev. Pl. Physiol.* **33**, 27–50.

Kirk, J.T.O. and Tilney-Bassett, R.A.E. (1978) in *The Plastids. Their Chemistry, Structure, Growth and Inheritance*, revised 2nd edition, Elsevier/North-Holland, New York, 219–241.

Preiss, J., Robinson, N., Spilatro, S. and McNamara, K. (1985) 'Starch synthesis and its regulation,' in *Regulation of Carbon Partitioning in Photosynthetic Tissue* (R.L. Heath and J. Preiss, eds.), Proc. Eighth Ann. Symp. Pl. Physiol., University of Riverside. Amer. Soc. Plant Physiol., Waverly Press, Maryland.

Stitt, M. (1985) 'Fine control of sucrose synthesis by fructose 2;6-bisphosphate,' in *Regulation of Carbon Partitioning in Photosynthetic Tissue* (R.L. Heath and J. Preiss, eds.) Proc. Eighth Ann. Symp. Pl. Physiol., University of Riverside. Amer. Soc. Plant Physiol., Waverly Press, Maryland.

Stitt, M. and Steup, M. (1985) 'Starch and sucrose degradation,' in *Encyclopedia of Plant Physiology, New Series*, Vol. 18, *Higher Plant Cell Respiration* (R. Douce and D.A. Day, eds.), Springer Verlag, Berlin, 347–390.

Index